UNIVERSITY   OF   NORTH   CAROLINA
STUDIES IN THE ROMANCE LANGUAGES AND LITERATURES
Number 81

OTHER VOICES: A STUDY OF THE
LATE POETRY OF LUIS CERNUDA

OTHER VOICES: A STUDY OF THE LATE POETRY OF LUIS CERNUDA

BY

ALEXANDER COLEMAN

CHAPEL HILL

THE UNIVERSITY OF NORTH CAROLINA PRESS

PRINTED IN SPAIN

DEPÓSITO LEGAL: V. 3.131 - 1969

ARTES GRÁFICAS SOLER, S. A. - JÁVEA, 30 - VALENCIA (8) - 1969

TABLE OF CONTENTS

Pages

PROLOGUE

This book began as a doctoral dissertation presented at Columbia University in 1964. It has since undergone innumerable and immensely helpful readings by many friends and a few adversaries, and I do hope that the resulting critical essay contains the best of what was there in the first place and a minimal amount of misunderstandings still remaining. Perhaps it is something close to a prior condemnation to admit that this book was originally a thesis; I don't know. But I can say that what began as an academic task ended as a revelation. This being so, it is difficult for me to describe rationally what the writing of this book meant to me while I was doing it —isn't it enough to say that reading Cernuda brought me to the essence of poetry? On a less exalted level, I would say the same for my readings in his criticism— I was never able to share his severe judgments of other contemporary Spanish poets of his generation, but even then, his negative ferocity was always illuminating to me, never merely destructive.

My book is thus nothing more than modest evidence of my reading Cernuda's late poetry, written after 1936. I make no pretensions to having made an exhaustive thematic study, and I would be foolish were I to have attempted it, since *that* book has already been written in a magnificent fashion: *"Et In Arcadia Ego": A Study of the Poetry of Luis Cernuda,* by Philip Silver. I would be very honored if my essay might be considered as complementary to Silver's incomparable study of Cernuda's thematics. My preoccupation throughout the book is both technical and emotional: the suppression of the subjective in the poetry, and the concomitant elaboration of objective, "dramatic" voices which define the trajectory between the first and third persons, the lyric and the dramatic.

My debts to friends and teachers are few but heavy. I still recall with gratitude the infinite spiritual generosity of Ángel del Río, exemplary teacher and mentor. My thanks also to Francisco García Lorca, whose intuitions regarding Cernuda and his poetry were of such utility to me. Gonzalo Sobejano gave unstintingly of his time and talents — whatever merits the book might have are quite frankly ascribable to his discerning and rigorous criticisms. And finally, a word of thanks to Luis Yglesias of Brandeis University, whose offhand mention of the "three voices in poetry" one hot afternoon in Cambridge gave me the initial idea for my study.

A. C.

New York City
June 12, 1968

ABBREVIATION USED IN THIS WORK:

RD, and page number; *La realidad y el deseo.* Cuarta edición, aumentada. México: Colección "Tezontle," Fondo de cultura económica, 1964. Copyright 1958.

I

ARS POETICA

In 1935, just prior to the publication of the first edition of
what was to become his only book of poetry, *La realidad y el
deseo*, successively enlarged through the years, Luis Cernuda
reluctantly attempted to define the impulse which governed his
poetic instinct. It is an important text, since it describes in
simple terms the alienation and solitude so characteristic of the
life and poetry of Cernuda, and from this the almost involuntary
ferment which brought forth the poetry.

> El instinto poético se despertó en mí gracias a la percep-
> ción más aguda de la realidad, experimentando, con un
> eco más hondo, la hermosura y la atracción del mundo
> circundante. Su efecto era, como en cierto modo ocurre
> con el deseo que provoca el amor, la exigencia, dolorosa
> a fuerza de intensidad, de salir de mí mismo, anegán-
> dome en aquel vasto cuerpo de la creación. Y lo que
> hacía aún más agónico aquel deseo era el reconocimiento
> tácito de su imposible satisfacción. A partir de entonces
> comencé a distinguir una corriente simultánea y opuesta
> dentro de mí: hacia la realidad y contra la realidad, de
> atracción y de hostilidad hacia lo real. El deseo me lle-
> vaba hacia la realidad que se ofrecía ante mis ojos como
> si sólo con su posesión pudiera alcanzar certeza de mi
> propia vida. Mas como esa posesión jamás la he alcan-
> zado sino de modo precario, de ahí la corriente contra-
> ria, de hostilidad ante el irónico atractivo de la reali-
> dad... Así pues, la esencia del problema poético, a mi
> entender, la constituye el conflicto entre realidad y deseo,
> entre apariencia y verdad, permitiéndonos alcanzar algu-
> na vislumbre de la imagen completa del mundo que

ignoramos, de la "idea divina del mundo que yace al fondo de la apariencia", según la frase de Fichte. [1]

The poet lies at the center point between contradictory forces, a mediator, so to speak, between the world of things and the soul. How essential it is, then, to retain a balanced middle way, to remain "attached" to the world of objects. It is a fragile relation, because its substance is an emotive force on the poet which Antonio Machado calls a "bond of feeling" (lazo cordial). Cernuda will insist upon the critical and logical faculties of the poet over the dubious gifts of imaginative fancy. The world must not indiscriminately invade the poet. Quite the contrary: the poet must give to the world through his art a new perception of the meaning of reality: Antonio Machado's words are so apt here:

> Cuando el poeta duda de que el centro del universo está en su propio corazón, de que su espíritu es fuente que mana, foco que irradia energía creadora capaz de informar y aun de deformar el mundo en torno, entonces, el espíritu del poeta vaga desconcertado nuevamente en torno a los objetos. El poeta duda ya de sus valores emotivos, y ante esta desestima del sujeto cae en el fetichismo de las cosas... Las cosas se materializan, se dispersan, se emancipan del lazo cordial que antes las domeñaba, y ahora parecen invadir y acorralar al poeta, perderle el respeto, reírsele en las barbas. En medio de una imaginería de bazar, el poeta siente su íntimo fracaso, se ríe de sí mismo, y, en consecuencia, tampoco prestará a sus creaciones otro valor que el de juguetes mecánicos, buenos, cuando más, para curar el tedio infantil. [2]

Cernuda laughed at himself frequently, but never because of the futility of his mission as a poet. He sensed the need for a bond between the world and the artist, no less than the need to preserve the distance between them. Desire impels us away from the soul toward reality; the final step in this process is a catastrophic one, oneness with the universe being at the same time an anihilation of the self. Roethke had a more ironic view of the conflict: "I can't marry the dirt." But with Cernuda, this

---

1   Luis Cernuda, *Poesía y literatura* (Barcelona, 1960), pp. 196-197.

2   Manuel y Antonio Machado, *Obras completas* (Madrid, 1957), p. 1220.

distance has implications for society also. Cernuda's world is full of people seen and loved, Society enters rarely, History never. In this he inherits a furtive tradition which he sensed in an intuitive fashion while a child and which was later confirmed by reading Rimbaud and Baudelaire. "En general, el poeta moderno, quiero decir el poeta que vive y escribe después de la etapa literaria romántica, ha roto con la sociedad de que es contemporáneo: ruptura donde nada violento hay, sino que se consuma quieta y tácitamente, y ésa es quizá la razón, no la supuesta oscuridad de su poesía, para que la sociedad no guste de ella: porque ya no se reconoce en la obra del poeta." [3]

Cernuda was a bitter observer of himself, his country, and his contemporaries. His critical faculties, both as spectator of his own inner life and that of others, retain a prejudiced and rancorous acumen which never relents even when directed to himself or his poetry. This characteristic appears, for instance, when he speaks of his unhappy adolescence while a student at the University of Seville. "Un mozo solo, sin ninguno de los apoyos que, gracias a la fortuna y a las relaciones, dispensa la sociedad a tantos, no podía menos de sentir hostilidad hacia esa sociedad en medio de la cual vivía como extraño." [4] A deeply rooted sense of alienation and solitude from what would superficially seem to be an inviting and amiable student life points to the young poet's conciousness of his own singularity, all while exacerbating an innate quarrel with those around him. Cernuda's rancor has had an undue effect upon his literary reputation, a fact that shouldn't surprise anyone who is familiar with the *ad hominem* criticism which has been directed toward Cernuda. There are other factors to consider. Luis Cernuda was born in Seville in 1902, attended the University there, and finally left Spain for England in the heat of the Civil War. In 1947 he accepted a professorship at Mount Holyoke College, where he remained until 1952. At that time he moved to Mexico City where he lived until his death in 1963. This exile from Spain was bound to affect all those who were forced to take it up. But there is another kind of exile, that of

---

[3] Luis Cernuda, *Estudios sobre poesía española contemporánea* (Madrid, 1957), pp. 199-200.
[4] Cernuda, *Poesía y literatura*, p. 242.

the "inner exile," still within the borders of Spain. This was the case with the young Cernuda. His geographical exile was a confirmation in reality of a spiritual state which had already fully crystallized while still a youth in Spain.

Cernuda's poetry is very much one of estrangement, nostalgia, and exile. He was destined to become a permanent stranger to Spain. It is a disservice, however, to reduce his sense of nostalgia to a uniquely geographical plane — narrow and exclusive conclusions about the poetry result all too readily. Cernuda's exile must be seen as incidental, in spite of the shattering effect that it must have had upon his life. His inner self, already so divided from within and divorced from others, underwent only an intensification of the many dualities and contradictions which he carried about him wherever he went. That sense of exile while still in Spain was instinctive at first, but soon his literary readings under the guidance of Pedro Salinas at the University of Seville aided him in a slow process toward a self definition and a justification of spiritual exile, to which he adhered in an, at times, tiresome fashion all through his life. "In (Cernuda's) lexicon the word *soledad* means not merely aloneness but separateness, absolute and terrifying. His is an ontological solitude, an acute awareness of his particular separateness from the world and the other finite creatures in it." [5] He should be removed, then, from a particular geographic locale. He recently to an excessively provincial view of his own poetry in a short poem from *Desolación de la quimera*, Part XI of *La realidad y el deseo*.

> Cuando allá dicen unos
> Que mis versos nacieron
> De la separación y la nostalgia
> Por la que fue mi tierra,
> ¿Sólo la más remota oyen entre mis voces?

That paradisal Eden which is present so often in the poetry written before the Spanish Civil War should not be considered as a manifestation of provincial *Sehnsucht*, but rather an elaboration of a fully conceptualized paradise. Man can only fall from

---

[5] Philip Silver, *"Et In Arcadia Ego": A Study of the Poetry of Luis Cernuda* (London, 1965), p. 43.

this Eden: "Pero terminó la niñez y caí en el mundo." [6] In order to grasp the full stature of Cernuda, he must be taken out of the circumstances which brought him forth. The world is very much present in his poems, but it is there and valid only when it is symbolic of a human situation.

The central issue is still the figure of the poet, his intent, his view of the poet's role in society. The contemporary poet's relation to his audience is at best a tenuous one — the search for the reader inevitably reduces itself these days to a quest for communion with the single reader, all hope lost for a charismatic dominion over the mass through the poetic word. The efficacy of commitment disdained, the poet senses himself divorced from society, having no place in the infernal machine. The artist embodying what Henry James called "the civic imagination" exists now only as a pallid shade in the realms of Stalinist social realism. The poet's previous alliance to the aristocracy and the courts precluded the necessity or even the possibility of his being "one" with society. He could lash the world, and he did. In the twentieth century, the aristocratic ideal is now in the hands of the poet himself, with Rilke and Mallarmé as imperious mentors. This devotion to the craft of poetry is not blandly Olympian, however; there remains the obligation to embody truth, though not necessarily in action. The exemption of the artist from the workaday world gave the Post-Romantic poet a sense of divine power; Cernuda follows in the tradition of Rimbaud and Baudelaire, an omnipotence that is best described as a willful effort to raise the artist-poet above the state of a merely sentient being.

The poet, Cernuda maintains, approaches the Divinity in that he unifies the diversity and flux of the world into a single vision; he senses the acute trials of humanity in any epoch and assumes the burden of expressing the suffering of those who are unable to "speak."

> Soy divino rescate a la pena del hombre,
> Forma de lo que huye de la luz a la sombra,
> Confusión de la muerte resuelta en melodía.

> (*RD.*, p. 144.)

---

[6]   Luis Cernuda, *Ocnos* (London, 1942), p. 43.

This is the *voyance* which the poet must possess. Assuming a divine perspective, he views the world in its totality, intuitively grasps the essential themes and preoccupations that are only vaguely apprehended by ordinary man.

> Contemplación, sosiego,
> El instante perfecto, que tal fruto
> Madura, inútil es para los otros,
> Condenando al poeta y su tarea
> De ver en unidad el ser disperso,
> El mundo fragmentario donde viven.
>
> (*RD.*, p. 226.)

Poetry must relate to the human condition, although its maker is foreign to humanity: a connection must be found that is central to the reader, a fully rounded human image must arise from the poetry, almost in spite of the tragic isolation of the poet. But he too, like the Divinity, has the obligation of taking on the sufferings of man in spite of the contempt and disdain accorded the poet — this is very much in the order of things. The burden which he carries is consciousness itself, a melancholy watchfulness about the fate of man on earth. Only the artist-poet protests against the injustice of man's condition. "Hero, pariah, martyr or satanic figure, it is the artist who stands alone and challenges God by usurping his place. In a world of shadows, chaos and flux, only the artist attempts to stem the flow toward non-being. But, if the exalted mission that Cernuda has described for himself and his fellow artists is anachronistically Romantic, there is nothing derivative in the impulse that has moved him to the creation of the portrait of the artist." [7]

> Amo el sabor amargo y puro de la vida,
> Este sentir por otros la conciencia
> Aletargada en ellos, con su remordimiento,
> Y aceptar los pecados que ellos mismos rechazan.
>
> (*RD.*, p. 224.)

These words are spoken by the man in the dialogue poem "Noche del hombre y su demonio," where the poet defends his transcen-

---

[7] Silver, *A Study*, pp. 181-182.

dental role against the contemptuous lack of comprehension of the devil-daemon. The poet, in Cernuda's view, can never uphold the values of the ordinary man. He must approach the Divinity with his art, serving as opposite to the moral collapse to which the devil invites him. The poet's superiority has nothing to do with morality — it can almost be described in terms of spatial elevation. He is proud, lonely, above men in the perspectivist sense. He has a broader view while contemplating incidentals. This kind of poet senses the power lines of an epoch, plunges to the essential spirit of the times. It is just this ability to see beyond, this comprehension and expression of a spiritual experience of a civilization that makes of him what he envisions himself to be — a poet. No matter how chaotic or attractive the world, the poet rises above it. His aim is unity and concordance, bringing together those seemingly endless series of opposites which characterize the life of the imagination when confronting the reality of the world. The title, *La realidad y el deseo*, points to one of the most striking polarities that summarizes his ever-present formulative conflicts. Similar to one of Cernuda's preferred philosophers, Heraclitus, the poet has within him a striving toward unity and oneness of the universe as perceived with the aid of the imagination. In a telling passage from his autobiographical essay, Cernuda meditates on the poet's singular need and sensitivity to the infinite varieties of human experience:

> Unas palabras de Empédocles, aunque desligadas de su sentido original, referente según creo a la transmigración de las almas, "porque antes de ahora he sido un muchacho y una muchacha, un matorral y un pájaro, y un pez torpe en el mar", me parecen expresar a maravilla esa sucesión varia y múltiple de experiencia y conocimiento que el poeta requiere, a falta de la cual su obra resulta pálida y estrecha. En mi caso particular, el cambio repetido de lugar, de país, de circunstancias, con la adaptación necesaria a los mismos, y la diferencia que el cambio me traía, sirvió de estímulo, y de alimento, a la mutación. [8]

---

[8] Cernuda, *Poesía y literatura*, p. 252.

With change, one becomes what one is not, a being is left behind with a particular set of circumstances, a new being awaits the spirit in another country. In English poetry, the archetypal figure for the poet-narrator who is "above" everything and beyond the self is Tiresias, the speaker and general overseer in T. S. Eliot's "The Waste Land." Eliot's figure contains the same kind of superhuman succession of lives; Tiresias is a figure which approaches the state of the Divinity in that he sees all experience and private points of view as one. This is so because he sees them all from a point outside — he is the eye of God. Eliot's footnote is interesting:

> Tiresias, although a mere spectator and not indeed a "character" is yet the most important personage in the poem, uniting all the rest. Just as the one-eyed merchant, seller of currants, melts into the Phoenician Sailor, and the latter is not wholly distinct from Ferdinand, Prince of Naples, *so all the women are one woman, and the two sexes meet in Tiresias.* What Tiresias *sees,* in fact, is the substance of the poem. [9]

The poet is the final result of an artificial consciousness, one that is beyond the capability of singular man; he is a construction of one image and situation after another. Since in Cernuda the personal and subjective perspective is not at all primary, he must represent the outer limit of man's consciousness, he must somehow escape the fixed point of view; just as Tiresias is everyone, the man Cernuda is an omnipresent citizen of everywhere.

The determination to avoid an unexamined and simplistic creative life has led the poet to speak of the need for a certain dynamism with regard to the self — it cannot be static, it must be incessantly in movement toward a further development, another incarnation. The *other* which is still to exist carries out the scrutiny of the being in the present. This inner perspectivism was characteristic of Baudelaire — as Sartre has said of him, "He was the man who never forgot himself. He looks at himself seeing: he looks in order to see himself looking." [10] This endless play of many

---

9   T. S. Eliot, "The Waste Land," in *The Complete Poems and Plays* (New York, 1952), p. 52.

10   Jean Paul Sartre, *Baudelaire* (Paris, 1947), p. 25.

selves within the self, what might be termed the division of the personality into divergent entities, of the many mirrors within the poet which reflect back upon himself, are all manifestations of the highest degree of consciousness. In Cernuda's poetry, any narcissistic fascination with the self never reaches a mental paralysis brought on by the self immobilized by its own image in the mirror. The symbolist cul de sac, a total stasis of being, is here replaced by a mobile searching for new selves through the use of monologues, *personae* other than the poet, who dramatize and express objectively an inner conflict which was initially subjective.

The role of the self is a recurrent preoccupation in Cernuda's poetry and literary criticism. The problem might be formulated in this way: how can objective validity be gotten from emotive, wholly personal experience? If the poet (not Cernuda in this case) believes that his self is the main concern in his poetry, then the poem will naturally center upon an "I." The "I" may well expand to cosmic proportions, as in Whitman — if the poet sits down, so does Jehovah; a door opens, it is the door to the universe. Still, that ever-expanding gyre is centered upon the being of the poet. Cernuda insisted upon an escape from the self into other selves and voices, but his insistence does not mean that this was always achieved. "...Yo mismo doy ocasión para una de las objeciones más serias que pueden hacerse a mi trabajo: la de que no siempre he sabido, o podido, mantener la distancia entre el hombre que sufre y el poeta que crea." [11]

This amounts to a strong suspicion about the role of personality in a work of art. Cernuda reveals something of himself when he comments upon Unamuno: "No sé si a otros ocurrirá, leyendo a Unamuno, ante aquella exhibición persistente de su "personalidad," apartar los ojos del libro, como suele hacerse para no ver un espectáculo repulsivo." [12] So too for Juan Ramón Jiménez:

> El carácter que en conjunto nos ofrece la obra de Juan Ramón Jiménez es el de un diario poético del autor... En realidad su yo está siempre sobre la escena, siendo

---

[11] Cernuda, *Poesía y literatura*, p. 279.
[12] *Ibid.*, p. 65.

éste quizá el único punto de contacto por el que se relaciona estrechamente con su generación, tan poco púdica en cuestiones de recato espiritual. Recuérdese el yo constante de Azorín, el yo, hombre de carne y hueso, de Unamuno. [13]

His objections to the all-encompassing ego of the writers of the Generation of '98 will lead him to enumerate a select list of authors in the Spanish language who offer what he finds to be a depersonalized poetry. Thus Jorge Manrique, Francisco de Aldana and Andrés Fernández de Andrada, author of the "Epístola moral a Fabio," are all exemplars of "cierta despersonalización, fundiendo al poeta con su medio de expresión, para que la voz, en vez de ser algo individual que suena bajo los harapos del fantoche que todos representamos, sea algo incorpóreo y desasido del accidente." [14]

An *other* is needed. For Cernuda, poetry should not be the monologue of a personality, but a created thing, an artificial poetic voice with which the *persona* may speak. Consciously literary language must be avoided. Cernuda's literary preferences are those which approximate his own ideal of calm, meditative speech. He found this idea in the English Metaphysical poets, in Wordsworth and Browning also. His affinity to spoken language in poetry was at first intuitive; as it was confirmed by his reading, it gradually became his credo as a poet. "Aprendí mucho de la poesía inglesa, sin cuya lectura y estudio mis versos serían hoy otra cosa, no sé si mejor o peor, pero sin duda otra cosa... si yo busqué aquella enseñanza y experiencia de la poesía inglesa fue porque ya la había encontrado, porque para ella estaba predispuesto." [15]

This meditative poetry, where the word serves only to express and to limit the thought, found an avid student in the young poet who took up residence in England in 1938. The affinity was a close one: "Pronto hallé en los poetas ingleses algunas características que me sedujeron: el efecto poético me pareció mucho más hondo si la voz no gritaba ni declamaba, si se extendía reiterándose, si

---

13 Luis Cernuda, "Juan Ramón Jiménez", *Hijo pródigo* (June, 1943), p. 153.
14 *Ibid.*, p. 154.
15 Cernuda, *Poesía y literatura*, pp. 259-260.

era menos gruesa y ampulosa." [16] What is striking is the use of elocutionary terminology in referring to poetry. It is indicative of one of Cernuda's many obsessions — poetic language must be very near colloquial speech. In Spanish poetry, Manrique serves as a good example of the laconic and quiet language which Cernuda prefers: "Su austeridad y su reticencia han hallado pocos adeptos en nuestro lirismo subsiguiente, y no es de extrañar, dada la afición vernácula a la redundancia y al énfasis." [17] The tradition of Manrique and Aldana, Cernuda feels, was revived in Spanish letters by Unamuno. In effect, what Unamuno achieved was nothing less than the return of poetic thought to Spanish verse. To this end he approached the work and the spirit of Leopardi, Wordsworth, Coleridge, Browning and Hölderlin. In this stern brand of poetry, visual or aural impressions are abandoned, the natural world functioning only as a trope to carry the import of the underlying idea. [18]

Thus the radical actuality of physical objects is not presented in an idle or passive way. The presence of things in the poem is the natural basis for the poet's higher ordering of experience. So too for the emotions of the poet. They are not directly, not to say mechanically, transmitted to the page, but transformed, not just "expressed." For this reason, the impressionism which Cernuda notes in the work of Juan Ramón Jiménez is condemned for a lack of objectivity towards the self. With unordered and impulsive revelation of the self, a poem is no longer evidence of the unifying powers of the poet's imagination, following Coleridge, but a simple manifestation of chaotic receptive powers. In order to get below the appearances, to relate things within the imagination, the poet must objectify his impressions and emotions. According to Cernuda, Jiménez lacked a critical view of his own self: "(El impresionismo) subsiste en él porque... responde a otro rasgo principal de su carácter: el subjetivismo egotista. Jiménez rara vez ha mostrado curiosidad intelectual por sorprender lo que haya

---

[16] *Ibid.*, p. 261.
[17] *Ibid.*, p. 60.
[18] A complete discussion of this point can be found in the excellent essay by José Ángel Valente, "Luis Cernuda y la poesía de la meditación," *La caña gris* (Valencia), pp. 29-38.

bajo la apariencia; ese atenerse a sus impresiones, ese conocer por sensaciones le bastó siempre." [19] This mistrust of personal sensitivity is typical of the mature Cernuda. But his quarrels with his contemporaries are not limited to this point. He severely criticizes his former teacher Pedro Salinas for other reasons. According to Cernuda, Salinas' error lay in the misuse of his own facility and ingenuity. Commenting upon Salinas' work, Cernuda describes him as "... un poeta ingenioso de tendencias cosmopolitas, llegando, si no a desconocer enteramente su naturaleza poética propia, casi hasta malograrla." [20]

Poetry as "play" or *conceptismo interior,* to use Leo Spitzer's description of Salinas' poetry, is alien to Cernuda. He advocates a fidelity between the inner man and the poetry, an organic bond between the world observed and the man, and finally a union between the philosophical conceptions of the poet and its expression in poetry. In any case, a sportive wielding of objects or a simple instinctive ecstasy before the world is anathema to him. Poetry is valid only when feeling is subjected to the logical faculty, where the thought expressed relates separate identities, and not just the rich diversity of passive fancy. This notion of poetry brings the world to a single vision; it is a refusal to allow chaos to destroy the effort to pattern and to order experience. The world must be held at a distance. "Aprendí a evitar, en lo posible, dos vicios literarios que en inglés se conocen, uno, como *pathetic fallacy* (creo que fue Ruskin quien le llamó así), lo que pudiera traducirse como engaño sentimental, tratando de que el proceso de mi experiencia se objetivara, y no deparase sólo al lector su resultado, o sea, una impresión subjetiva; otro, como *purple patch* o trozo de bravura, la bonitura y lo superfino de la expresión, no condescendiendo con frases que me gustaran por sí mismas y sacrificándolas a la línea del poema, al dibujo de la composición. Ya se recordará cómo, en general, mi instinto literario tendía a prevenirme contra riesgos tales." [21] Ruskin's definition is relevant to Cernuda's instincts; in *Modern Painters* he made the now classic distinction between "the ordinary, proper and true appearances

---

[19] Cernuda, *Estudios,* p. 123.
[20] *Ibid.,* p. 201.
[21] Cernuda, *Poesía y literatura,* p. 261.

of things to us; and the extraordinary, or false appearances, when we are under the influence of emotion, or contemplative fancy; false appearances, I say, as being entirely unconnected with any real power or character in the object, and only imputed to it by us." [22] As Cernuda said of Jiménez, "...ese atenerse a sus impresiones, ese conocer por sensaciones le bastó siempre."

The objects of the world should never determine the poem, but should be subservient to the philosophical imagination, and not the fancy. The poet envisioned by Cernuda is one who correlates and objectifies. This association of sensibility was concisely defined by Unamuno: "Piensa el sentimiento, siente el pensamiento." [23]

The language of poetry is governed by the ideal which it serves. An organic bond between thought and feeling dictates, or at least would indicate, the suitability of the plain, flat cadences of ordinary speech. Oddly enough, Cernuda cites the witty adage of Juan Ramón on this point: "Quien escribe como se habla irá más lejos en lo porvenir que quien escribe como se escribe." [24] Cernuda himself devised a suggestive theory concerning the relation between colloquial and literary language which is most relevant here. "1) Hay momentos cuando lenguaje hablado y lenguaje escrito coinciden, como ocurre en las *Coplas* de Manrique; 2) otros cuando lenguaje hablado y lenguaje escrito comienzan a divergir, como ocurre en Garcilaso; y 3) otros, por último, cuando lenguaje hablado y lenguaje escrito se oponen, como ocurre en Góngora." [25] Cernuda's preference clearly lies with the first "moment." His petulant attacks against the work of other poets are at times unfounded and unfair, but surely he and the greatest of his contemporaries and his predecessors would be in agreement in preferring plain, colloquial language, whether it be Unamuno, Machado, Jiménez, Salinas or Guillén. But Cernuda finds strange affinities — he praises Campoamor, for instance, in the following way: "...su mérito principal: haber desterrado de

[22] John Ruskin, *Modern Painters* (New York: n.d.), III, p. 154.
[23] "Credo poético," in *Antología poética* (Madrid, 1942), p. 7.
[24] As cited in Cernuda, *Estudios*, p. 123.
[25] *Ibid.*, p. 17.

nuestra poesía el lenguaje preconcebidamente poético." [26] Such a "poetic" language is pernicious to true expression, since clichés carry far too much semantic weight beforehand, that is, before the creative act. All the poetry of Cernuda orients itself around two poles — the submission of the poetic word to the thought and the equilibrium between spoken language and written language. Although Cernuda's vocabulary is relatively constricted and the poetry itself abounds in flat apthegms and "prosaic" rhythms, the final breakthrough to the colloquial was never accomplished, and perhaps it is just as well. Nowhere in the collected poems can the garrulous and unbridled speech of a Browning be found, even though the latter is often cited by Cernuda as a supreme example of the use of the *persona*.

But what of the poem itself? How does it extend itself from the object observed to an idea? The mental process involved has rightly been termed "meditative poetry" by Louis L. Martz, and his definition applies to Cernuda's poetic practice:

> A meditative poem is a work that creates an interior drama of the mind; this dramatic action is usually... created by some form of self-address, in which the mind grasps firmly a problem or situation deliberately evoked by memory, brings it forward toward the full light of consciousness, and concludes with a moment of illumination, where the speaker's self has, for a time, found an answer to its conflicts. [27]

The "problem or situation" is a human one — the poet must speak in human terms to humans, just as Aldana or Manrique spoke to their jaded contemporaries. Cernuda is content as they were to present the world in its disappointing finitude, its plainness, and then bring his imagination to play on what he has perceived. There are no easy ways to insight.

In English and American poetry, we have come to recognize and appreciate a plain, unrhetorical language, exemplifying concision of style which matches the simple naming of unadorned things. The poetic diction is thus severely attenuated — Cernuda

---

[26] *Ibid.*, p. 35.
[27] Louis L. Martz, *The Poetry of Meditation* (New Haven, 1955), p. 330.

has already said in another connection that in his opinion dryness *(sequedad)* is one of the best qualities that a poem can have.

In the regretful questioning of Manrique before the spectacle of the world's mutability, in Unamuno's uncertainty before Velazquez' Christ, in Cernuda's plaintive celebration of the spirit of Greece, we sense the underlying power of a pensive and measured poetic speech which is truly *una honda palpitación del espíritu.*

II

HÖLDERLIN AND CERNUDA

Cernuda's desire for a tensive integration of things and beings into a single world view, his insistence upon a balance between the polarities pointed up by the conflict between reality and desire, impelled him to seek out other poets having some kind of affinity with this ideal. Cernuda's interest in the poetry of Friedrich Hölderlin brought about, by the poet's own admission, a new direction to his poetry, a metamorphosis of old techniques into a new practice. His study of Hölderlin, done with the aid of a young German poet residing in Madrid, resulted in well-intentioned but inaccurate translations of a few of Hölderlin's greatest poems. Cernuda's reading of the German poet at that time is a particularly fortunate instance of fruitful spiritual communion, for it so happens that many of Hölderlin's characteristic spiritual beliefs became a part of Cernuda's major phase, the poetry written after 1936. Cernuda has always had much of the elegiac poet in him; this trait is now to be intensified, along with a more generous and catholic selection of poetic materials and a newly-found transcendental vision of the world.

So often literary influences seem to be invented by critics and unknown to the author supposedly influenced — in the case of Hölderlin and Cernuda, the latter acknowledges with the fervent devotion of a disciple the tutelage and spiritual example of the German Romantic. Cernuda was then (1935) in the process of completing his book "Invocaciones"; he had finished the poem "El joven marino," but had not gone any further. Just then he took up the study of Hölderlin; the next poem in the collection, the "Himno a la tristeza," shows a heavy and impressive debt to Hölderlin. Just as the book "Invocaciones" marks the final culmination of an initial stage in the poetry of Cernuda, so too "El joven marino" marks the last of a series of poems of similar themes, such as "Cuerpo en pena" or "A un muchacho andaluz." In a passage from his autobiographical essay, Cernuda describes his own reaction to the work of Hölderlin, and its effect upon the poems written after "El joven marino."

> En 1935 comencé a componer los poemas de "Invocaciones a las gracias del Mundo", título que, en la edición tercera de *La realidad y el deseo*, quedó reducido a "Invocaciones", por llegar a parecerme engolado y pretencioso. Al comenzar dichos poemas, cansado de los poemitas breves a la manera de Machado y Jiménez, poetas que habían perdido quizá el sentido de lo que es composición, percibí que la materia a informar en ellos exigía mayor dimensión, mayor amplitud; al mismo propósito ayudaba el que por entonces me sintiera capaz (perdóneseme la presunción) de decirlo todo en el poema, frente a la limitación mezquina de aquello que en los años inmediatos anteriores se llamó poesía "pura". Fuera cuales fueran los efectos benéficos de aquella pretensión a decirlo todo en el verso, efectos entre los cuales me permitiría indicar el de ampliar mis límites de la experiencia poética, que los "puros" redujeron hasta el enrarecimiento, en mi caso hubo, además, por torpeza mía, uno perjudicial: hacerme divagar no poco, sobre todo al comienzo de ciertos poemas en dicha colección. Se nota también, en el tono de los mismos, ampulosidad; de ahí que me parezca absurda la pretensión de algunos de que "El joven marino" sea el poema mejor que yo haya escrito. En realidad si les parece así es a causa de esos dos efectos que acabo de indicar, garrulería y ampulosidad, que tan característicos son de nuestros gustos literarios tradicionales.
>
> Más que mediada ya la colección, antes de componer el "Himno a la tristeza", comencé a leer y a estudiar a Hölderlin, cuyo conocimiento ha sido una de mis mayores experiencias en cuanto poeta. Cansado de la estrechez en preferencias poéticas de los superrealistas franceses, cosa natural en ellos, como franceses que eran, mi interés de lector comenzó a orientarse hacia otros poetas

de lengua alemana e inglesa, y, para leerlos, trataba de estudiar sus lenguas respectivas. [1]

Hölderlin directed Cernuda to a contemplative verse that soon became characteristic in his later work. Cernuda's comments show considerably more than the occasional interest of a translator. "Al ir descubriendo, palabra por palabra, el texto de Hölderlin, la hondura y hermosura poética del mismo parecían levantarme hacia lo más alto que pueda ofrecernos la poesía. Así aprendía, no sólo una visión nueva del mundo, sino, consonante con ella, una técnica nueva de la expresión poética. Los poemas que entonces traduje aparecieron en *Cruz y raya* a comienzos de 1936." [2]

Hölderlin was a seer and something of a mystic who saw, or rather attempted to impose, unity and order onto the structure of the universe. As the most consummate expression of this impulse, Hölderlin returned to the Greek world of myths, gods and heroes where there was not only a harmony between man and nature, but between the gods and man. Cernuda was attracted to this idea of the chain of being. Henceforth, the ideal of unity and harmony will govern much of Cernuda's poetic practice, a tendency which was intensified by his readings in Diels's *Fragmente der Vorsokratiker* while at Mount Holyoke. The fusion of the individual existence with the universe gives the poet a vicarious and fleeting mastery over change; he continually projects his own self into Nature in a vain attempt to lose himself in it and so escape man's fate. Cernuda commented lucidly on Hölderlin in his preface to the *Cruz y raya* translations: "Mas en esos poemas... hay siempre un impulso armonioso y luminoso que el paganismo encauzó y al cual prestó expresión." [3] But Cernuda is not just an idle antiquarian — this vision is an important one to him, for it seems to be the only one possible in an age without faith; a pantheism, then, on the broadest scale imaginable. "What above all Hölderlin admired in ancient Greece (or in his own image of it) was its perpetual awareness of Divinity — the fact that every human activity was in some way hallowed and consecrated. This

---

1 Cernuda, *Poesía y literatura*, pp. 252-253.
2 *Ibid.* p. 254.
3 *Cruz y Raya*, XXXII (1935), p. 116.

ever-present sense of Divinity, this harmony between man and Nature, was what Hölderlin found most wanting in his own materialistic, departmentalized and dehumanized age; and to express his own ever-present sense of Divinity, to remind men of the gods they seem to have forgotten, was what he took to be his chief mission as a poet." [4] This consciousness places the poet above other men, nearer the gods —Heidegger's term for Hölderlin is "Hinausgeworfener"— one who has thrown himself out and above others; he places him in "jenes Zwischen zwischen den Göttern und den Menschen . . . ," that intermediary state between the gods and man. [5] This is consonant with Cernuda's ideal. Both poets place themselves above men, but like Christ are crucified and sacrificed. The effect of Hölderlin upon Cernuda is not easy to describe. Certainly, Cernuda's world vision is expanded, Nature now appearing to him in an intense, almost magical way. The basis of his poetry is altered — it tends toward an increasing objectivity and generalized depersonalization of thematics. The poetry more often than not escapes from the poet's self entirely. Naturally, there is no definitive demarcation within the collection of poems entitled "Invocaciones"; even with the earlier poetry in the collection, there is some tendency toward non-subjective thematics, poems speaking of melancholy, solitude or the nature of existence. Still, the direction of Cernuda's art definitely alters in the last two poems of the book, "Himno a la tristeza" and "A las estatuas de los dioses." In these there is a more objectified expression, the poet now sees himself not at the center of the universe, but rather as a mere function in time. As his egotism decreases under the weight of this new world perspective, his transcendental consciousness expands. There is a more disciplined mastery over the resources of language, a calm and impassive poetic voice, a new dramatization of situations. The embodiment of his desire, rather than being mankind, is now the whole cosmos as represented in the natural world.

---

[4] *Hölderlin: Selected Poems*, Trans. J. B. Leishman, with an introduction. (London, 1954), p. 4.

[5] Martin Heidegger, *Erläuterungen zu Hölderlins Dichtung*, (Frankfurt, 1951), p. 43.

The contemplation of Nature, assuming an ever-increasing role in the late poetry, can only be understood in the light of the poet's own spiritual affinities. For him, Nature is beyond time and suffering, truly beyond good and evil. It is totally positive, it always says yes: it is man who has invented the restrictive negative, the "Thou shalt not." In its totality, it encompasses all flux and resolves the anguish of change. The poet allies himself to it not only as a sign which points out his destiny on earth, but as a fatal attempt to unite himself with it so as to stay the change effected upon him by time. Above all, Nature goes beyond the either-or principle and coalesces all its elements into unquestioning oneness; this non-exclusiveness so desired by Cernuda becomes a recurrent desire, for his own impulse tends toward the principle of "both-and," toward the fusion of the disparate elements of the world.

The structure of the last two poems from "Invocaciones" gives us an indication of the direction which the later poetry will take. This in turn is inevitably governed by the kinds of experience which move the poet to write; his choice of themes, his increasing tendency to derive analogies and correspondences from the topic. The archetypal late poem of Cernuda might begin with a brusque opening statement which is then exemplified in ramification and ultimate consequences. Once the object is named, be it a flower, a tree or the Escorial, the poet then meditates upon its relation to himself, tries to delve into what he can learn from it. The poetry is didactically formulated: if the topic is animate, the poet is often reminded of the past and of what is decaying or in flux before his eyes. If inanimate, the poet might attempt to bind his spirit to the deathless immutability which it represents. Either technique is elegiac in the end. The poem might then end with a concluding group of symbols or images which conciliate the experience and compress its meaning in a final abstraction.

The "Himno a la tristeza" offers us the first example of the new direction which Cernuda's poetry was to take after his reading of Hölderlin. The title itself recalls the many hymns of Hölderlin, not to mention the single poems of Keats, Shelley and Coleridge on the same topic. The opening of Cernuda's ode:

Fortalecido estoy contra tu pecho

thrusts us immediately *in medias res,* in vivid contrast to the lazy divagation of the earlier poems in the collection. Here, the poem commences in a forthright and assertive way, with no preliminary artifice. It brusquely announces a combative feeling, and indirectly defines the character of the mythical protagonist that is Melancholy. Cernuda's new style demands this dramatic opening device with no verbal ornament. The use of the participle as the opening word of the first line might have been suggested to Cernuda by his own Hölderlin translations, where such phrases as the following occur:

> Abiertas las ventanas del cielo
> Y libre el genio de la noche ...
> or
> Alejándose de la tierra esas leyendas ...

The participle is strengthened by the reversal of the participle, intensifying the percussive effect of the final syllable:

> fortalecido estoy.

The strophe continues in the same tone of aggressive complaint:

> Fortalecido estoy contra tu pecho
> De augusta piedra fría,
> Bajo tus ojos crepusculares
> Oh madre inmortal.

The images of immobility and rigidity immediately bring to mind the effects of melancholy upon the human spirit. The figure addressed is clearly of monumental proportions in the imagination of the poet, and its remoteness is intensified by the impersonal stare of the "ojos crepusculares." The diminution of the poet's physical size is conveyed by the preposition "bajo"; the speaker and the object are hardly equals. The poet does not content himself with further introspection into the nature of melancholy. He immediately seeks out its cause: the impassivity of the universe to man's plight, the ultimately vain struggle of man to fortify himself against the tragedy of each individual life, his helplessness before the passage of time. In Cernuda's view time does not pass, it "slips by":

> Desengañada alienta en ti mi vida,
> Oyendo en el pausado retiro nocturno
> Ligeramente resbalar las pisadas
> De los días juveniles, que se alejan
> Apacibles y graves, en la mirada,
> Con una misma luz, compasión y reproche;
> Y van tras ellos, como irisado humo,
> Los sueños creados con mi pensamiento
> Los hijos del anhelo y la esperanza.

The poet's image of the even flow of time is represented in the poem by the technical devices of enjambment and the avoidance of interruptive punctuation. The "resbalamiento" ascribed to time is emphasized by the imperceptible flow of the thought from one line to another:

> Oyendo en el pausado retiro nocturno
> Ligeramente resbalar las pisadas
> De los días juveniles, ...

In contrast, the poet in the succeeding lines will halt the train of thought repeatedly in order to force us to pause and judge the effect of remembrance of past time which is now being noted. In another poet, the punctuation of the following lines might well seem excessive:

> (Los días) ... que se alejan
> Apacibles y graves, en la mirada,
> Con una misma luz, compasión y reproche;
> Y van tras ellos, como irisado humo,
> Los sueños creados con mi pensamiento,
> Los hijos del anhelo y la esperanza.

The tempo of our reading is subtly controlled for poetic emphasis or expressive design.

The original flat apothegm has undergone further development; melancholy is defined as an inevitable response to the contemplation of time passing. The qualities of impassivity ascribed to melancholy in the first strophe are now applied to time itself. The reaction of the poet points to the real cause — the mutability of things, the passage of youth, the futile effort to recapture lost experience. The characterization of melancholy as "madre inmortal" is not fortuitous, for the nostalgic dreams of the past are now termed "los hijos del anhelo y la esperanza." The adjectives in turn are utilized by Cernuda in a distinctive way. They serve to retard the rhythm of our reading, and give a marmorial heaviness to the lines. The symmetrical modification of the noun inevitably slows our reading. In the present poem, numerous examples can be found:

> augusta piedra fría
> pausado retiro nocturno
> renovado encanto verdeante
> celeste donadora recóndita
> polvorienta agua salobre
> alta gloria resplandeciente
> remota tierra misteriosa.

In each case, the noun is placed between two adjectives, and in some cases the rhythmic stress is identical in each of the words:

> pausado retiro nocturno

The silence of the universe before the condition of man is not total, in Cernuda's view. The gods are not entirely vindictive towards man. In this poem they acquire a compassion, since the solitude which they afford men is a healing one.

> La soledad poblé de seres a mi imagen,
> Como un dios aburrido;
> Los amé si eran bellos,
> Mi compañía les dí cuando me amaron,
> Y ahora como ese mismo dios aislado estoy,
> Inerme y blanco tal una flor cortada.

The creation of beings in the poet's imagination is compared to the human beings engendered by the ancient gods. The notion of a slack and irresponsible divinity coincides with the figure of the idle and useless poet. The elevated, semi-divine perspective of the speaker divorced from humanity by solitude affords him mastery over men, but his solitude will always be a melancholic one.

> Olvidándome voy en este vago cuerpo,
> Nutrido por las hierbas leves
> Y las brillantes frutas de la tierra,
> El pan y el vino alados,
> En mi nocturno lecho a solas.

The sixth strophe returns to the direct address used earlier. Instead of the combative spirit of the first strophes, the restorative power of solitude is described with a calmer tone. The thought of the lover sitting before the window is directed to his lost happiness. The distance in time between the remembered act and the observer's presence is effectively conveyed by the three prepositional phrases inserted between subject and predicate, making "la dicha perdida" all the more distant.

> Al amante aligeras las atónitas horas
> De su soledad, cuando en desierta estancia
> La ventana, sobre apacible naturaleza,
> Bajo una luz lejana,
> Ante sus ojos nebulosos traza
> Con renovado encanto verdeante
> La estampa inconsciente de su dicha perdida.

A similar effect is used in the later poem "A las estatuas de los dioses":

> En tanto el poeta, en la noche otoñal,
> Bajo el blanco embeleso lunático,
> Mira las ramas que el verdor abandona ...

The renewal of experience through memory and retrospection is elaborated even further in the next strophe:

> Tú nos devuelves vírgenes las horas
> Del pasado; fuertes bajo el hechizo
> De tu mirada inmensa,
> Como guerrero intacto
> En su fuerza desnudo tras de broquel broncíneo,
> Serenos vamos bajo los blancos arcos del futuro.

It is here that the initial epithet given to melancholy begins to undergo a gradual transformation. The adjectives "fuerte" and "inmenso" recall the usage in the first strophe, "...tu pecho de augusta piedra fría . . . ," but the "ojos crepusculares" have now attained a larger benevolence, already suggested in the previous strophe:

> ... ...
> Pero tú, celeste donadora recóndita,
> Nunca los ojos quitas de tus hijos
> Los hombres, por el mal hostigados.

The figure of the poet is now introduced:

> Viven y mueren a solas los poetas
> Restituyendo en claras lágrimas
> La polvorienta agua salobre ...

The poet, more than any other man, clamors for the healing powers of melancholy, since it impels him to fix his eyes on beauty and to glorify it, the unique role of the artist. Still addressing this personification, he asks,

> ¿Quién sino tú cuida sus vidas, le da fuerzas
> Para alzar la mirada entre tanta miseria,
> En la hermosura perdidos ciegamente?
> ¿Quién sino tú, amante y madre eterna?

In preparation for the final summation and climax of the poem, Cernuda invites the figure to view the spectacle of degraded humanity in a passage that reminds us of Pablo Neruda's hortatory supplications to his readers, such as

> Ven conmigo a la sombra de las administraciones
> or
> Examinemos ahora los títulos y las condiciones... [6]

Cernuda's lines have a similar ring:

> Escucha cómo avanzan las generaciones
> Sobre esta remota tierra misteriosa;
> Marchan hostigados los hombres
> Bajo la yerta sombra de los antepasados...

---

[6] "Desespediente," in *Obras completas* (Buenos Aires, 1956), p. 185.

> Y el cuerpo fatigado se reclina
> Sobre la misma huella tibia
> De otra carne precipitada en el olvido.

A question, answered by the last two lines of the poem, finally reveals to us the ultimate intent of the poet. Far from challenging the inhuman power of melancholy as he did initially, he ultimately recognizes compassion as a gift which strengthens men in their distress:

> ¿Dónde floreces tú, como vaga corola
> Henchida del piadoso aroma que te alienta
> En las nupcias terrenas con los hombres?
> No eres hiel ni eres pena, sino amor de justicia imposible,
> Tú, la compasión humana de los dioses.

> (*RD.*, pp. 122-125.)

There is a progression which gives the poem its form: the effort on the part of the poet to derive broader implications from the initial statement. Cernuda, by means of variation and alteration of motifs, directs his thought to larger and greater meaning as the poem develops. It is interesting to note the direction of the poem. Beginning with the personification of melancholy as cold stone, an antagonist of man, the poem culminates with a radiant nuptial act of the goddess with man. The repellent frigidity that the poet ascribed to the figure is finally denied by the poet. As for the emotions, the poet's initial bravura contrasts sharply with the newly-achieved serenity.

"A las estatuas de los dioses" is even more indicative of Hölderlin's influence. Cernuda's prologue to his translations are of interest. Many of the ideas contained in the note reappear in Cernuda's original poem. He begins in a nostalgic and evocative temper:

> La época en que le tocó vivir a Hölderlin nos presenta un mundo heroico, agitado por profundas conmociones históricas, surcado brevemente con radiantes vidas juveniles, apagadas antes de llegar al mediodía, como el destino de los mancebos mitológicos. Su destino, en cambio, pasa oscuro y enigmático, oponiéndose fatalmente a la llama que animaba aquel cuerpo.
> ...Algunos hombres, en diferentes siglos, parecen guardar una pálida nostalgia por la desaparición de aque-

llos dioses, blancos seres inmateriales impulsados por
deseos no ajenos a la tierra, pero dotados de vida inmortal. Son tales hombres imborrable eco vivo de las
fuerzas paganas hoy hundidas, como si en ellos ardiese
todavía una chispa de tan armoniosa hoguera religiosa;
eco sin fuerza ya, pero que tampoco puede perderse
por completo. Y la misma dramática aptitud para participar, aun débilmente, en una divinidad caída y en un
culto olvidado, convierte a esos seres mortales en seres
semi-divinos perdidos entre la confusa masa de los humanos. Tal fué el caso de Friedrich Hölderlin... Dos
héroes, sin embargo, se nutrieron con su ignorada vida:
Hiperión y Empédocles; el héroe juvenil y el héroe que
divisa la vida sobre dos iguales vertientes. Héroes ven-
cidos, es verdad, como su creador; mas con derrota que
la muerte convierte en victoria... Una demoníaca fuerza
aniquilaba a Hölderlin por el fuego, fuego que al propio
tiempo lo salvaba. [7]

For Cernuda, the poet is the unique being who is alone capable
of celebrating the highest ideals of man, which in turn found
their most noble manifestation in the world of Greek mythology.
"El amor, la poesía, la fuerza, la belleza, todos estos remotos
impulsos que mueven al mundo, a pesar de la inmensa fealdad
que los hombres arrojan diariamente sobre ellos para deformarlos
o destruirlos, no son simples palabras; son algo que aquella reli-
gión supo simbolizar externamente a través de criaturas ideales,
cuyo recuerdo aún puede estremecer la imaginación humana." [8]

Cernuda considered Hölderlin to be the exemplary poet. The
fact that his heroes, Hyperion and Empedocles, now stand defeated
indicates the fate of "the sense of the divine" before the levelling
power of contemporary life. But this defeat can be turned into
victory. Cernuda does not wish to represent an anachronistic
nostalgia, but he does endeavor to reawaken, as did Hölderlin,
the sense of the divine in Nature by revivifying the mythological
world. In the poem "A las estatuas de los dioses," Cernuda
reinstates the symbolic intent of the mutilated statues with a fervor
that brings back, if only fleetingly, a pre-Christian age of belief.

---

[7] *Cruz y Raya,* XXXII (1935), pp. 115-117.
[8] *Ibid.,* p. 115.

The poem elaborates even further the implications contained
in the prefatory essay to the Hölderlin translations. Similar to the
"Himno a la tristeza," this opens with a direct address to the gods:

> Hermosas y vencidas soñáis,
> Vueltos los ciegos ojos hacia el cielo,
> Mirando las remotas edades
> De titánicos hombres,
> Cuyo amor os daba ligeras guirnaldas
> Y la olorosa llama se alzaba
> Hacia la luz divina, su hermana celeste.

Much of the language derives directly from Cernuda's reading of
Hölderlin. The adjective "titánico," not present in any previous
poem of Cernuda, recalls Hölderlin's "Die Titanen;" the "luz
divina" is directly related to one of Hölderlin's recurrent symbols,
"das himmlische Feuer." The final line of the above-quoted strophe
expresses the idea of harmony of all elements in the universe that
Hölderlin sensed so well: "la luz divina" is the "sister" of the
"olorosa llama." All things of the world are seen as images of a
higher state of being. The poet, contemplating the statues in their
present state, reverts the temporal focus of the poem to ancient
times, and then describes the end of the belief that engendered
them:

> La miseria y la muerte futuras
> No pensadas aún, en vuestras manos
> Bajo un inofensivo sueño adormecían
> Sus venenosas flores bellas,
> ... ...
> Hoy yacéis, mutiladas y oscuras,
> Entre los grises jardines de las ciudades,
> Piedra inútil que el soplo celeste no anima,
> Abandonadas de la súplica y la humana esperanza.

He then asks them not to return to the earth of our day, but rather

> Impasibles reinad en el divino espacio.
> Distraiga con su gracia el copero solícito
> La cólera de vuestro poder que despierta.

The final strophe follows the structure of the "Himno a la tristeza." The observer contemplates the fate of the statues, compar-

ing them to the still living belief which they represent. In opposition to "hoy yacéis, mutiladas y oscuras, / Entre los grises jardines de las ciudades," the poet sees far off the distant yet blinding light of the golden throne of the gods.

> En tanto el poeta, en la noche otoñal,
> Bajo el blanco embeleso lunático,
> Mira las ramas que el verdor abandona
> Nevarse de luz beatamente,
> Y sueña con vuestro trono de oro
> Y vuestra faz cegadora,
> Lejos de los hombres,
> Allá en la altura impenetrable.

> (*RD.*, pp. 125-126.)

At the end of the poem, where the golden light is perceived by the poet, there is a climatic moment which is repeated by Cernuda in later poems. For instance, in the first poem of his next book *Las nubes,* the poem "Noche de luna" has a conclusion which is touched with the calm emptiness and silence of the cosmos:

> ... Definitivamente frente a frente
> El silencio de un mundo que ha sido
> Y la pura belleza tranquila de la nada.

> (*RD.*, p. 131.)

In the same collection, the poem "A Larra con unas violetas" ends with a meditation on poetry which has a similar physical ascension as a climax:

> ... Es breve la palabra como el canto de un pájaro,
> Mas un claro jirón puede prenderse en ella
> De embriaguez, pasión, belleza fugitivas,
> Y subir, ángel vigía que atestigua del hombre,
> Allá hasta la región celeste e impasible.

> (*RD.*, p. 142.)

The integration of thought and word so evident in these two poems stems not from an artificially imposed "economy of words," but rather from an instinctive poetic impulse finally brought fruition. Hölderlin's influence is capital in this regard, not only in the vocabulary and in the choice of epithets, but in the structure of the poetic meditation. The contemplation of Nature, the calm objectivity in viewing the world are both introduced into Cernuda's poetics as fundamental reorientation that will govern future practice. The objective themes divert Cernuda's poetic voice from a simplistic and intuitive expression to the creation of another voice — that is, one that is not his own, and which is in reality a dramatic projection of himself into another character. Thus, this poetic voice assumes the form of a dramatic monologue or dialogue which is almost theatrical in its intensity.

III

NATURE AS SYMBOL

Las nubes, the collection written between 1937 and 1949,
contains a considerable number of Nature poems of a meditative
and objective character. Cernuda's poetic evolution is here marked
by a search for poetry of the "non-I," and to this end the world of
things offers itself to him, at once alluring and repellent, as is all
which is outside the self and which cannot be encompassed
by it. Here Nature is more than a passive observer of Humanity; it
is a touchstone for the poet's contemplation of his existence; only
through the wholly *other* can man see his own life on earth. The
lesson learned from Nature is a stern one, but there is more than
a little of the stoic in Cernuda in any case; his affinitive authors
and philosophers tend to view the course of human existence fully
conscious of the mutability of things but still reluctant to protest
too much about it. Through Nature, Cernuda conveys his acute
sense of helplessness before the passage of time: ever changing
and advancing, Time stays with the world, but men are condemned
to a single portion of it. The natural world reflects the poet's own
anguish, for its own obliviousness to temporality presages the
quietude, stillness and death of the mortal once again reunited
to Nature.

The poet turns from the world of society, its passions and
its ephemerality, and seeks in Nature not only greater permanence
in a world of flux, but also a sign which points to his own
destiny. In the rapid cycles of life and death in Nature the
poet sees a compressed and foreshortened representation of
the fate of living things. The contemplation of beauty in Nature

is removed from the realms of aestheticism — in Cernuda this contemplation is a recognition and a lament for the fate of Nature. "El poeta, pues, intenta fijar la belleza transitoria del mundo que percibe, refiriéndola al mundo invisible que presiente, y al desfallecer y quedar vencido en esa lucha desigual, su voz... llora enamorada la pérdida de lo que ama." [1] The function of poetry is emphasized once again; it is a search for what Cernuda terms "the hidden truth," that is, the lesson which each object in Nature contains. Cernuda's imagination always feeds on the particulars of the world, deriving larger consequences from seemingly scattered details. All reality offers itself to him, but his selection and ordering of it, his own meditation upon the meaning of what he has perceived is carried out by his philosophically oriented imagination. Nature not only is, but it means something.

The poem "Cordura" is a good example of Cernuda's disposition to see Nature in a synechdochic fashion, not only as an indication of another reality but also as a focus for his own thought. Whether viewing a landscape or a flower, Cernuda's habit is to open the poem with a flat descriptive statement naming the subject of the poem (in this case, an English landscape late in the afternoon) and add, in a selective manner, additional elements. In this poem, the first line is immediately broadened in intent by the activation of the "campo amortecido," which in effect forms the subject of the succeeding three lines. This personification intensifies the effect that winter is soon to have upon the trees.

---

[1] Cernuda, *Poesía y literatura,* pp. 199-200. Cernuda's late poetry reveals an obsession with both fixation and flux — if we are reminded of Heraclitus, it is a very just memento of that philosopher's massive influence upon Cernuda. In the same way, Cernuda's commentators inevitably take on a glow that is both Heraclitean and Platonic. Thus: "Lo que concede sólido sustrato al término *realidad,* en la antinomia que da título a sus poesías completas, es algo de más honda dimensión que la realidad concreta de la hermosura corpórea y tangible, y aun de su abstracta idealización. Es, en última instancia, la evidencia de esa misma hermosura como realidad fluyente, que existe no más para desaparecer, temporal en el único sentido bajo el cual a los humanos les es dado concebir el tiempo. Y alzado frente a ella, como imposible, un *deseo* tenso de fijación, de permanencia, de eternidad, que la mente del hombre sólo puede vislumbrar como condición suprema del lado trascendente, invisible y simultáneo de aquella misma realidad." José Olivio Jiménez, *Cinco Poetas del Tiempo* (Madrid, 1964), p. 102.

> Suena la lluvia oscura.
> El campo amortecido
> Inclina hacia el invierno
> Cimas densas de árboles.

The enumeration of what is seen, nothing more, continues unrelieved in the second stanza; the "prosaic tone" remains unchanged.

> Los cristales son bruma
> Donde un iris mojado
> Refleja ramas grises,
> Humo de hogares, nubes.

The adjectivization has been carefully regulated so as to heighten the physical obscurity of the landscape. Each line contains a noun or adjective to this purpose: in the first strophe we find *oscura, amortecido, invierno, densas*. This attenuation of light is intentional, for the poet, seeking an analogy in Nature to convey the nostalgia for the lost Eden of his youth, so different from the countryside of Surrey in the winter, immediately relates the thought to a happenstance: the appearance of light through the clouds.

> A veces, por los claros
> Del cielo, la amarilla
> Luz de un edén perdido
> Aún baja a las praderas.

Here is a correspondence between his own nostalgia and a natural phenomenon. From this, the poet draws broader meanings. The effect of the thought, accentuated and confirmed by the ray of light, leads the poet to enlarge and elaborate the effects of nostalgia upon himself, an exile.

> Un hondo sentimiento
> De alegrías pasadas,
> Hechas olvido bajo
> Tierra, llena la tarde.

Nature so depicted cannot be imagined in total stillness and silence for long. The poet introduces new sonoral elements that intensify the retrospection that was first sensed when the ray of light appeared through the clouds. These sounds are the calling of some crows and the voices of the men working the fields in the distance.

> Turbando el aire quieto
> Con una queja ronca,
> Como sombras, los cuervos
> Agudos, giran, pasan.
>
> Voces traquilas hay
> De hombres, hacia lo lejos,
> Que el suelo están labrando
> Como hicieron los padres.

Their voices remind Cernuda of the brusque contrast between himself and other men. They are rooted to their land, their families and their country in an ancient bond, but the poet is a solitary exile. The men live with hope, warmth and oneness with their environment, whereas the poet's condition is that of the stranger living uniquely through memory.

> Sus manos, si se extienden,
> Hallan manos amigas.
> Su fe es la misma. Juntos
> Viven la misma espera.

The alienation of the poet, his "otherness" from all around him, intensifies the vision of his own singularity. In anticipation of the final strophes, this isolation is explored in more detail.

> Todo ha sido creado,
> Como yo, de la sombra:
> Esta tierra a mí ajena,
> Estos cuerpos ajenos.
>
> Un sueño, que conmigo
> Él puso para siempre,
> Me aísla. Así está el chopo
> Entre encinas robustas.

The solitude of one among many, the inability to possess, all receive a startling image in the following strophe — "la cruz sin nadie"; that is, the desired self-sacrifice of the solitary figure for the sake of another is destined to remain unrealized, a vain hope. That communion among men that is exemplified by the life of the laborers in the field is now symbolized by the light that contrasts with the oncoming dusk:

> Duro es hallarse solo
> En medio de los cuerpos.
> Pero esa forma tiene
> Su amor: la cruz sin nadie.
>
> Por ese amor espero,
> Despierto en su regazo,
> Hallar una alba pura
> Comunión con los hombres.
>
> Mas la luz deja el campo.
> Es tarde y nace el frío.
> Cerrada está la puerta,
> Alumbrando la lámpara.

The defeat of light by the overpowering force of the oncoming night, the door closed to the world, the artificial light that replaces the natural, all point to the poet's isolation. The desired repose, communion and warmth among men endure only as an ideal. Nature regains its dominion over man; the wind echoes the solitude of the poet.

> Por las sendas sombrías
> Se duele el viento ahora
> Como alma aislada en lucha.
> La noche será breve.
>
> (RD., pp. 155-157.)

Although it would not be just to derive final conclusions from the close analysis of one poem, certainly Cernuda's usage of Nature is very close to that of the Romantic tradition, wherein inner states of mind were correlated with Nature itself. For this reason, Nature, in Cernuda's poems, has a selective character that stems from the final intent of the poet.

In a later poem from *Como quien espera el alba,* similar elements of Nature are utilized to intensify the thought. The poem

"Tarde oscura" begins with a metaphysical conceit in which "sueño" and "niebla" serve as dividers of the self and the world.

> Lo mismo que un sueño
> Al cuerpo separa
> Del alma, esta niebla
> Tierra y luz aparta.

Here the potentiality in Nature is immediately exploited: "lo mismo" assures us that the two dividing elements are simply operating on different planes of the universe, but do not contradict themselves. The implied transcendence of the two functions, however, is made clearer in the next strophe, for the effect of the "niebla" has an analogous effect upon the microcosm that is the poet:

> Todo es raro y vago:
> Ni són en el viento,
> Latido en el agua,
> Color en el suelo.
>
> De sí mismo extraño,
> Sabes lo que espera
> El pájaro quieto
> Por la rama seca?

The division within the self actuated by the "sueño" is transferred to the inanimate bird, a sense of immanence and foreboding implied in the rhetorical question. The double function of "sueño" and "niebla" are now clearer: their effect upon man and his world is revealed as premonitions of death—deathly tranquility, abulia. The heartbeat is the only indication that life and time are still passing:

> (Yace) La vida, y tú solo,
> No muerto, no vivo,
> En el pecho sientes
> Débil su latido.

The final strophes constitute the poet's solution to this paralysis —a gratuitous act of the will that seeks out a community of light and faith. This illumination is to be understood in the widest sense possible, for it applies as much to the physical realities previously described as to the poet's own consciousness. Again, it is a question of alternate juxtaposition and division of varying levels of experience within one poem. The poet, occupying the purely human perspective, extends beyond himself and makes little distinction between the particular and the universal.

> Por estos suburbios
> Sórdidos, sin norte
> Vas, como el destino
> Inútil del hombre.
>
> Y en el pensamiento
> Luz o fe ahora
> Buscas, mientras vence
> Afuera la sombra.
>
> (*RD.*, pp. 198-199.)

In the last two poems, selective aspects of Nature are manipulated so as to represent the poet's inner state. Against a prevailing silence and latency, he introduces sharp contrasts of light or sound, a "shock" which leads him to derive further implications from his contemplation. In such poems, the simple enumeration reminds us of a similar technique in the shorter poems of Antonio Machado. In the following poem of Cernuda, Machado's influence is felt not only in the adjectivization, but also in the vague sense of melancholy brought on by the oppressive dusk:

> Ahora, al poniente morado de la tarde,
> En flor ya los magnolios mojados de rocío,
> Pasar aquellas calles, mientras crece
> La luna por el aire, será soñar despierto.
>
> El cielo con su queja harán más vasto
> Bandos de golondrinas; el agua en una fuente
> Librará puramente la honda voz de la tierra;
> Luego el cielo y la tierra quedarán silenciosos.
>
> En el rincón de algún compás, a solas
> Con la frente en la mano, un fantasma
> Que vuelve, llorarías pensando
> Cuán bella fue la vida y cuán inútil.
>
> (*RD.*, p. 208.)

Here, the sky and the swallows act as the "interrupting force" which directs the poet's thought to the mutability of things. Nature is a docile master and teacher of the poet. Its lesson is one of forebearance and secular asceticism. There is something of the anchorite in Cernuda; he repeatedly admonishes himself to heed the lesson learned. The spectacle before him tells him to seize the day, eternalize the moment. "Aquí la definición es inevitable y se nos presenta casi fatalmente: la poesía fija a la belleza efímera." [2]

An important poem in this regard is "Los espinos;" the poet has written that this poem is one of his preferred, for it conveys a total experience with a minimum of words. "...Lo mismo que en el relámpago, basta un instante para su iluminación, sólo hay que trasladar lo esencial de la experiencia. Así creo que ocurrió en "Los espinos", uno de mis poemas preferidos." [3] The essence of experience is conveyed here by a masterful use of synecdoche, making the part stand for the whole:

Verdor nuevo los espinos
Tienen ya por la colina,
Toda de púrpura y nieve
En el aire estremecida.

Cuántos ciclos florecidos
Les has visto; aunque a la cita
Ellos serán siempre fieles,
Tú no lo serás un día.

Antes que la sombra caiga,
Aprende cómo es la dicha
Ante los espinos blancos
Y rojos en flor. Vé. Mira.

(RD., p. 212.)

The meditation is based upon a simple declarative statement of what the poet sees. Brusquely, without transition, the poet ruminates on the eternal return of Nature and the finite condition of humanity that observes it. The conclusion in the last lines of the

---

2 Cernuda, *Poesía y literatura*, p. 199.
3 *Ibid.*, pp. 270-271.

poem derives not only from just looking at Nature, but also from
the realization that man's fate is divergent from that of the natural
world. Time is meaningless to Nature, but it is of the essence to
man. What else can man do, then, but compromise? The order of
the world cannot be thwarted. The only path for the intelligent
man is to seize the moment of felicitous vision, not to let it slip
by. The exhortation to the poet by the poet is impelled by the
power of time over man and its impotence over Nature.

The contemplative poem of Cernuda should be viewed as
a mirror of the mutability of existence. In many poems, the poet
approaches Nature in order to bind himself more completely to
unfeeling creation. In so doing he confounds the passage of time
and attains an immortality through this bond, a salvation through
things; but it is an ultimately futile one, since the poet is fully
aware of the *engaño* that is the basis of the universe. The union
of beings with things, a fusion of these two parts of the world, is
nothing if not an attempt to be more than one is. Sensing the
unconscious and unquestioning repose of Nature, its infinite
contentment to remain what it is without complaint, the poet
embarks on this vain quest fully aware of his final destiny. Cernuda
sees in Nature the image of himself and those around him.
However, there are degrees of mutability, different rates of decay.
Nothing is ever totally dead or alive, each object and being
contains the apportionment due it. Man alone complains of his,
demands to be other than his station in life permits him. Cernuda's
effort to alter the terms of his own life leads him to unusual
assessments of some elements of Nature: for instance, his affinity
and love for trees goes well beyond mere aesthetic rapture. The
tree stands as the prime example of timelessness while still
containing life — an element which lives while containing within
it total contradiction. In Casalduero's words, "El árbol es un dios
que, hundido en la tierra y vibrante en el aire, convierte la sed
en forma: hojas, movimiento, sombra, juego de ramas, y encuentra
la justificación de su pasión en la unidad vital que hace de él lo
que él es." [4] Trees have always been obsessive to Cernuda. His

---

[4] Joaquín Casalduero, *Cántico de Jorge Guillén* (New York and Madrid, 1953), p. 47.

affection for them brought him to write three poems about trees, each one different from the other. One of them, "Otros aires," tries to describe his curiosity about the New World before leaving England. "...Mi pregunta acerca de la nueva tierra se cifró así: "¿cómo serán los árboles aquéllos?", que daría el verso primero para un poema ("Otros aires") escrito luego en Mount Holyoke. "No se extrañe que en los árboles cifrara, inconscientemente, la curiosidad hacia el país aún desconocido, porque ante mí tuve todos aquellos años los hermosos, los bellísimos árboles ingleses: robles, encinas, olmos."[5] Cernuda ascribes a soul to them which is the soul of man brought back to life. This is the poem "El chopo."

> Si, muerto el cuerpo, el alma que ha servido
> Noblemente la vida alcanza entonces
> Un destino más alto, por la escala
> De viva perfección que a Dios le guía,
> Fije el sueño divino a tu alma errante
> Y con nueva raíz vuelva a tierra.
>
> Luego brote inconsciente, revestida
> Del tronco esbelto y gris, con ramas leves,
> Todas verdor alado, de algún chopo,
> Hijo feliz del viento y de la tierra,
> Libre en su mundo azul, puro tal lira
> De juventud y amor, vivo sin tiempo.
>
> (RD., p. 219.)

The aspiration to eternity through metamorphosis is another variation of the basic *sed de eternidad*. The tree is the quasi-eternal object of this striving, for it is alive, almost free from temporal limits. The poet endeavors to extend his being by projecting it into the tree, embracing it and making himself part of the permanence and non-flux of Nature.

The most extensive poem on the subject is, fittingly, "El Árbol," dedicated to an old tree in the garden of the Fellows of Emmanuel College in Cambridge, England. Without containing

---

[5] Cernuda, *Poesía y literatura*, p. 269.

the metaphysical impulse toward union that was found in the previous poem, it intensifies the concept of the tree as outside of time, free of *el engaño mortal*. This idea is reinforced in our consciousness by the physical presence of youth seated beneath the tree. The tree and the youths are the antithesis to one another.

> Al lado de las aguas está, como leyenda,
> En su jardín murado y silencioso,
> El árbol bello dos veces centenario,
> Las poderosas ramas extendidas,
> Cerco de tanta hierba, entrelazando hojas,
> Dosel donde una sombra edénica subsiste.

Its timelessness pervades the observer, too, for he willingly lets time go by while resting under the tree. These moments are a last echo of an ideal and never-ending existence: Adam must have had a similar longing:

> Bajo este cielo nórdico nacido,
> Cuya luz es tan breve, e incierta aún siendo breve,
> Apenas embeleso estival lo traspasa y exalta
> Como a su hermano el plátano del mediodía,
> Sonoro de cigarras, junto del cual es grato
> Dejar morir el tiempo divinamente inútil.

The relation of this tree to those of Eden is suggested by the use of the noun "hermano" which recalls the lost paradise of his youth in Seville. The appearance of the youths under the tree signals the beginning of the meditation:

> ... Son entonces los días, algunos despejados,
> Algunos nebulosos, más tibios de este clima,
> Sueño septentrional que el sol casi no rompe,
> Y hacia el estanque vienen rondas de mozos rubios:
> Temblando, tantos cuerpos ligeros, queda el agua;
> Vibrando, tantas voces timbradas, queda el aire.

Against the figurative immortality of the tree, the poet now contrasts the ages of man in contrast to those of the tree. Youth is judged to be a "temporary" state of immortality. Free (as it were) from the bondage of time, it is totally oriented toward the future. At the same time, it is heedless of the past and of the destructive effects of memory and nostalgia.

> Entre sus mocedades, vida prometedora,
> Aunque pronto marchita en usos tristes (.)
> ... ...
> Cuando la juventud el mundo es ancho,
> Su medida tan vasta como vasto el deseo,
> La soledad ligera, placentero ese irse,
> Mirando sin nostalgia cosas y criaturas
> Amigas un momento, en blanco la memoria
> De recuerdos, que un día serán fardo cansado.

For youth, solitude does not weigh as it will later; leaving familiar surroundings is not yet a heavy task. But these "immortals" are not alone in the world: the *others* ("los otros") still exist — those no longer young. In Cernuda's world, which is so reliant on the ideal of youth, "the others" are not adults or even the aged. They are simply those who have lost their youth, without necessarily having entered any other age "level." Humanity is thus divided in two. "The others" have been conquered by "usos tristes," which are the mortal enemies of the youthful impulse — routine, empty gesture, complacency before advancing age: in a word, limbo on earth.

> Atrás quedan los otros, repitiendo
> Sin urgencia interior los gestos aprendidos,
> Legitimados siempre por un provecho estéril;
> Ya grey apareada, de hijos productora,
> Pasiva ante el dolor como bestia asombrada,
> Viva en un limbo idéntico al que en la muerte encuentra.

Between these two divisions the poet interposes an imaginary figure, neither old nor young, which reminds us immediately of that epoch of life known to Dante as the "mezzo del cammin" and to Hölderlin as "Hälfte des Lebens."

> Pero ocurre una pausa en medio del camino;
> La mirada que anhela, vuelta hacia lo futuro,
> Es nostálgica ahora, vuelta hacia lo pasado; ...

Youth is illusory in the end, for this looking back is just another way of describing the "aging process," where the dynamic impulse toward hope and expectation doubles back upon itself irrevocably into contemplative remembrance and nostalgia. Youth is yet another *engaño* which must be mastered and overcome.

> Y el mozo iluso es viejo, él mismo ignora cómo
> Entre sueños fue el tiempo malgastado;
> Ya su faz reflejada extraña le aparece,
> Más que su faz extraña su conciencia,
> De donde huyó el fervor trocado por disgusto,
> Tal pájaro extranjero en nido que otro hizo.

The reflection of his own face is now alien to the former youth's conception of himself. He is not one of "the others." His idea of himself no longer conforms to reality and the fact that he is no longer young does not conform to his desire to be young. He is now a "mozo iluso," a "pájaro extranjero."

The poem ends with the timeless symbol of the tree. As was the case with "El chopo," the permanence of the tree symbolizes placid Nature which silently lives without complaint.

> Mientras, en su jardín, el árbol bello existe
> Libre del engaño mortal que al tiempo engendra,
> Y si la luz escapa de su cima a la tarde,
> Cuando aquel aire ganan lentamente las sombras,
> Sólo aparece triste a quien triste le mira:
> Ser de un mundo perfecto donde el hombre es extraño.
>
> (*RD.*, pp. 242-244.)

Language, syntax and subject have been gradually disciplined and dominated by the didactic sense of the poet. Particular objects are chosen over others because they carry the burden of the thought most efficaciously; the tree, for instance, fits the poet's intent by implying a new definition of death. While contemplating it, the poet loses his identity and binds himself to the animate immortality that it represents. This view of Nature receives its ultimate expression in the two exquisite poems about flowers, "Otros tulipanes amarillos" and "Violetas." The vital relation between beauty and nostalgia is immediately apparent, since Cernuda's meditation springs from the simple contemplation of the flower to a recalling of past years and remembered beauty. The first strophe of "Otros tulipanes amarillos" sets the "stage" and places the central "character."

> Primavera con niebla, amarga, sin perfume,
> De verde y gris tan vago tal si el halo
> De plata que la envuelve luz no fuera,
> Mas sueño; deshecha en lluvia leve
> Moja hierba y piedra, sobre la tierra anima
> Tulipanes dorados, cuyo color tan vivo
> Es como son perdido por el aire sordo.

The sight of the tulips inevitably recalls other flowers seen in the past; the meditation now progresses to include the passing of all experience, that of youth above all:

> ¿Dónde recuerdas tú de otra primavera,
> En otra tierra y tiempo, mojada como ésta
> Con lluvia leve, como ésta cifrada
> En otros tulipanes amarillos?
> Entonces algo más florecía, aunque no en tierra;
> En ti. Tanta luz amarilla duele ahora,
> O ¿no será recuerdo lo que duele?

The organic flowering of the tulips suggests a concordant growth in youth, but the continuum which the human body follows from youth to old age is not the same as that of Nature and the flowers in particular, for they die within a few months and are reborn every spring, thus attaining a kind of immortality through a repeated cycle of death. The human can never have the consolation of physical rebirth, although the poet's most conscious efforts have tended to infuse his own physical being into animate Nature. Immortality is achieved through this act of the will. The verb *florecer* takes on a dual sense here, both of growth along a terminal time continuum (man) and that of rapid "flowering" which renews itself each spring. The verse "...entonces algo más florecía, aunque no en tierra; / En ti..." reflects the fatal flowering of youth, whereas the verb as applied to the flowers themselves hardly has the same connotation of reminiscence and foreboding, for the flowers never demand from their creator a reason for their presence on earth — they simply fulfill what they have been made to be.

Spring is irrelevant to man; it invites our hopes for eternity, it incites us to believe in it momentarily and affords us the cycle of Nature as proof. But for man, the signs are false and the appearances have no fundamental basis in our world. As Eliot has said, "April is the cruellest month, breeding / Lilacs out of the dead land, mixing / Memory and desire,...." [6] So too for Cernuda:

> Es cruel la primavera joven, precipita
> Al hombre por el viejo camino de los yerros,
> Con ramas de cerezo florido lo enajena,
> Con viento del sur tibio lo extravía.

The concept of remembrance is an activation of lost pleasures and love. The tulips bring back to his mind the same clash of colors observed years before — yellow against grey:

> Así te vuelva hoy aquella sombra
> Lejana, que por una lejana primavera,
> También gris y amarilla, quiso amarte
> Con capricho egoísta, como el hombre ama
> En un mundo incompleto...

To the poet, the contemplation of the flowers forces him to acknowledge the incompleteness of the world. That is to say that it is incomplete for men, since their lives are never fully accomplished and brought to fruition: death severs the continuum which Nature alone possesses in its entirety. In transferring the cycle of life and death to flowers, the poet contrasts our assumption of permanence with the reality of flux. According to Cernuda, life *seems* to exist:

> Nuestra vida parece que está aquí: con hojas
> Seguras en su rama, hasta que nazca el frío;
> Con flores en su tallo, hasta que brote el viento;
> Con luz allá en su cielo, hasta que surjan nubes.

Nature has its own kind of eternity which appears each spring, but man can expect nothing but an abrupt termination of his

---

[6] T. S. Eliot, "The Waste Land" in *The Complete Poems and Plays* (New York, 1952), p. 37.

own life. The larger question of man's reason for existence is now explored, since death seemingly reduces human life to irrelevance and meaninglessness.

> ¿Qué empresa nuestra es ésta, abandonada
> Inútilmente un día? ¿Qué afectos imperiosos
> Éstos, con cuyos nombres se alimenta el olvido?
> Ya en tu vida las sombras pesan más que los cuerpos;
> Llámalos hoy, si hay alguno que escuche
> Entre la hierba sola de esta primavera,
> Y aprende ese silencio antes que el tiempo llegue.
>
> (RD., pp. 219-220.)

The ordered, closed world of the garden attracts Cernuda also. The following is the poem "Jardín," a touching example of Cernuda's meditative style.

> Desde un rincón sentado
> Mira la luz, la hierba,
> Los troncos, la musgosa
> Piedra que mide el tiempo
>
> Al sol en la glorieta,
> Y las ninfeas, copos
> De sueño sobre el agua
> Inmóvil de la fuente.
>
> Allá en lo alto la trama
> Traslúcida de hojas,
> El cielo con su pálido
> Azul, las nubes blancas.
>
> Un mirlo dulcemente
> Canta, tal la voz misma
> Del jardín que te hablara.
> En la hora apacible
>
> Mira bien con tus ojos,
> Como si acariciaras
> Todo. Gratitud debes
> De tan puro sosiego,
>
> Libre de gozo y pena,
> A la luz, porque pronto
> Tal tú de aquí, se parte.
> A lo lejos escuchas

La pisada ilusoria
Del tiempo, que se mueve
Hacia el invierno, Entonces
Tu pensamiento y este

Jardín que así contemplas
Por la luz traspasado,
Han de yacer con largo
Sueño, mudos, sombríos.

(*RD.*, pp. 194-195.)

Many of the elements of this poem are recognizable from the first poems analyzed in this chapter. For instance, the passage of time described as "la pisada ilusoria" recalls the "Himno a la tristeza," where a similar passage occurs:

... Oyendo en el pausado retiro nocturno
Ligeramente resbalar las pisadas
De los días juveniles...

(*RD.*, p. 122.)

For full possession, the objects need not be touched. In Cernuda, the culminating moment is always possession by sight — such verbs as *contemplar, ver* and *mirar* reoccur, whereas tactile verbs appear less frequently. The poet draws a conclusion which is at the same time an injunction to himself and his reader, dramatized by the use of the imperative tense. Such was the case with the poem "Los espinos."

Antes que la sombra caiga
Aprende cómo es la dicha
Ante los espinos blancos
Y rojos en flor. Vé. Mira.

The use of the second person, ostensibly a means of addressing the reader, might also be interpreted as a double of the poetic self, so that *tú* might mean either the reader or the poet. In any case, the described things become mirrors for the experience of the poet.

As is customary, the poem begins with the placement of the observer and an enumeration of what he sees, which are the elements of the garden that first meet his eye, placed as he is "desde un rincón sentado." If we examine the first four strophes and consider them as a unit in the form of a prelude, it is clear that the poet's eye naturally rises from the solid substantives of the garden, "...la hierba, / Los troncos, la musgosa / Piedra que mide el tiempo(,)" and gradually rises, as if it were the eye of a camera, from the ground to the skies. The second strophe cites "(el) sol en la glorieta," the third higher still with the peaks of the trees and then the open sky, "Allá en alto la trama / Traslúcida de hojas / El cielo con su pálido / Azul, las nubes blancas" and finally the voice of the bird, the sound of Nature, which immediately returns him to the garden. The poet cannot rest with a simple description of the reality that he sees. Once reality has been observed, the imagination of the poet then re-orders the experience in accordance with the thought to be expressed. A prelude is contained in the first four strophes, and the second four symmetrically conclude the poem with a meditation on what has only been observed in the first part.

The clearest indication that the poem has changed focus, having left behind the description of reality, is the fact that the vocabulary becomes almost completely unreal, and is only linked to the reality of the garden by the link in the poet's mind between what he has seen and what he is thinking about. The vocabulary is indicative: *gratitud, sosiego, gozo, pena, luz, pisada ilusoria.* Just as the diction takes on an new character, Nature itself undergoes a similar alteration. The poem begins with all evidences of summer and ends with a deathly vision of the garden without life. The use of the verb "yacer" is especially telling here — it brings a wintry premonition of death to the garden and to all men. The passage of time, which does not affect Nature since it is reborn each Spring, is immediately related to the observer and the reader by the use of this verb. This is the sleep of the dead, and not just dead Nature. The poem closes with a muting of the birdsong and a darkening of the sun which lit the garden in the first strophes.

In another poem, "Jardín antiguo," the same kind of placid observation of Nature is used for a rather different effect. The garden, contrasting with the locale in the previous poem which underwent a severe compression of time, now remains as it is throughout the poem. The alterations take place entirely within

the mind of the poet. No imaginative re-creation of Nature in
another season is used. Instead, an appreciation of what is seen
leads to a nostalgia for the past, and further, a desire to become
one with an order which is outside of time. Each strophe begins
with an infinitive, the progression toward feeling being a gradual
one: ir, oír, ver, sentir. This is in accordance with the poet's usual
practice to reserve the expression of inner states for the latter
part of the poem, where the sensory elements have been con-
templated.

> Ir de nuevo al jardín cerrado,
> Que tras los arcos de la tapia,
> Entre magnolios, limoneros,
> Guarda el encanto de las aguas.
>
> Oír de nuevo en el silencio,
> Vivo de trinos y de hojas,
> El susurro tibio del aire
> Donde las almas viejas flotan.
>
> Ver otra vez el cielo hondo
> A lo lejos, la torre esbelta
> Tal flor de luz sobre las palmas:
> Las cosas todas siempre bellas.
>
> Sentir otra vez, como entonces,
> La espina aguda del deseo,
> Mientras la juventud pasada
> Vuelve. Sueño de un dios sin tiempo.
>
> (RD., p. 166.)

The aural and visual elements that are recognized in the first
three strophes have had an intense effect upon the imagination,
for the fourth strophe is little more than a final summation of the
three different experiences into a single image. Again, what is
seen in the garden leads the direction of the thought to past
experience, *recuerdo* in the broadest sense. The fact that Nature
always points to that past should no longer surprise us, but it is
interesting to notice the reappearance in the last line of the idea
that the world is essentially an *engaño*. Beauty brings back the
past, or so it seems, but this re-living of past experience by memory
is illusory. As was the case with the previous poem the transparent

function of Nature as a reflector and example of the thought should be evident to the reader — very few things are cited, and there is a curious vacuity in the objects themselves, for the garden is totally still, the silence broken only by the trills of a bird. The sky is empty. It is almost as if the poet had created this emptiness in the poem only to fill it in his own way through the force of the imagination. In any case, Nature is described with few adjectives and a minimum of detail. It is severely abstract and selective, a garden after all.

Cernuda's search for eternity and permanence has led to a seizing of the objects in Nature in order to forge out of them an eternal consciousness which will carry him beyond the bounds of his own temporal existence and back into a timeless world of childlike innocence.

> With childhood and the child's experience of the world irrevocably lost and the experience of love in the world but an anguished and temporary respite, Nature itself —the same natural world that was the landscape of Eden— becomes, like the figure of the child, an objective embodiment, ever present in the fallen world of insatiable desire, of the innocence, purity and timelessness that was the child's mode of existence.... Nature embodies an insensate, reclusive ideal of existence in sharp contrast with the poet's own time-bound experience of the adult world of physical love. [7]

In contrast to a simplistic Romantic longing, Cernuda's alliance with things is not just directed toward the Infinite, for the elements of Nature in his poetry are rigorously ordered and manipulated so as to bring out this transcendence of the self. But this is a false transcendence, for the imposition of order upon Nature that the garden symbolizes is entirely dependent upon the action of the poet's will; the fusion of the poet with things ceases upon loss of consciousness, that is, the death of the poet. He must break out of himself while alive and attempt to alter the nature of things. In a sense, the rebirth that Cernuda strives for was actually

---

[7]   Silver, A Study, p. 130.

fulfilled in Unamuno's case, for the latter's own "thirst for eternity" was partially assuaged by the sight of his children, who would always carry with them part of him long after he died. But disregarding for the moment the degrees of fulfillment of this thirst, it must be recognized that the underlying drive is the same for both, for they find a salvation of their consciousness in that which they are not — Nature in the case of Cernuda, children in Unamuno's. The desire for rebirth and renewal of the self is thus a false kind of trascendence. It is possible, though, to view this otherwise. In going beyond what one is, the artist extends his whole being into another. In Cernuda's Nature meditations, we always sense the fragility of his outer self, his very real *pudor*. Nature takes on the character of an object exploited to prolong human existence. It is a manipulation, of course, and Cernuda does not limit this poetic play to Nature. His fascination with constructions of stone such as El Escorial and gothic cathedrals is indicative of the breadth of this desire for projection. Ortega's "Meditaciones del Escorial" is a guide to this new aspect of Cernuda's many extensions of the self; the next chapter considers this and other matters as examples of a further extension of Cernuda's mature poetic practice.

IV

THE SPIRIT IN STONE

In the Nature poems, the structural design was to specify and place the object within a setting which, in turn, was then elaborated and made relevant to the poet's own expressive design. This determined a meticulous selection of particular objects so that they might conform to the greatest degree to the thought that motivated the writing of the poem. A similar conformity of topic to thought can be seen in Cernuda's affinity to the Escorial and to cathedrals. Using these monuments as the center of his meditation, he reads into them a philosophical credo which serves as a solace and a guide to him, another goal for his incessant desire to be enveloped in things. What strikes us so markedly in Cernuda's affinity for the Escorial, for instance, is the fact that the edifice is a representation in stone of what Philip the Second imagined for himself and the Spain of his time. For Cernuda, the Escorial comes to represent an organic relation between the king, the people he represents, and this architectural summation of Spain in the throes of the Counter-Reformation. The transfiguration of the edifice has only a tangential basis in the object itself. It is recreated in the imagination of an exile at a considerable distance from what it really is. Thus this poem and the others in this chapter are *flawed allegories,* where the object named is neither itself nor reducible to a moral quality: rather, it is sign chosen by the poet to focus his meditation on the meaning of Spain. The poet views the Escorial as an immutable and eternal embodiment of the paradox of Spain. The title of Cernuda's meditation, "Ruiseñor sobre la piedra," points to the meaning of the monastery for Cernuda, for the nightingale functions as a symbol of mutability in contrast to the timelessness of the stone:

> Lirio sereno en piedra erguido
> Junto al huerto monástico pareces.
> Ruiseñor claro entre los pinos
> Que un canto silencioso levantara.
> Ó fruto de granada, recio afuera,
> Mas propicio y jugoso en lo escondido.

The inner and outer perspectives of the building diverge and contradict one another — our impression of the monastery is governed by the point of view from which we contemplate it. If the edifice has a formidable and fortress-like appearance, its interior contains bedchambers, gardens and libraries which are not indicated by its exterior. The comparison of the building to the fruit which contains a hidden delight is a perfect image for the whole of the Escorial. Its constituent qualities, once rendered through the image of the fruit, are then expanded and placed in a universal perspective:

> Así, Escorial, te mira mi recuerdo.
> Si hacia los cielos anchos te alzas duro,
> Sobre el agua serena del estanque
> Hecho gracia sonríes. Y las nubes
> Coronan tus designios inmortales.

The direction of the poem changes from a consideration of the object itself to a wider speculation about its meaning. Like Antonio Machado, who foresook his native Andalusia for Castile, Cernuda, while still conscious of the region of his youth, turns away from it in order to plunge to the essence of Spain, that "Castilla eterna" which is the true spiritual home of the poet:

> Recuerdo bien el sur donde el olivo crece
> Junto al mar claro y el cortijo blanco,
> Mas hoy va mi recuerdo más arriba, a la sierra
> Gris bajo el cielo azul, cubierta de pinares,
> Y allí encuentra regazo, alma con alma.
> Mucho enseña el destierro de nuestra propia tierra.

This union of the Castilian soul with that of the poet will later be complemented by the same desire transferred to the physical realm: "Y el cuerpo, que es de tierra, clama por su tierra." Thus the maternal image is almost complete, since the union and affection of the *alma y cuerpo* find a *regazo* in the remembrance of Castile and the Escorial — truly, *un hogar espiritual.* This fact established, the symbolic function of the Escorial is revealed by the structure of the poem itself, where, with almost no transition, the poet interchanges the figure of the Escorial in his imagination with that of Spain itself. Carrying the idea even further, the poet addresses Spain in a filial way, similar to Unamuno's continual personification of Castile as *una madre espiritual.* The final step in this gradual process toward the re-creation of the Escorial in the poet's mind takes place in the next strophe, but not before intensifying the contrast between the reassuring solidity of the imagined Escorial and the poet's present state of exile and solitude:

> Porque me he perdido
> En el tiempo lo mismo que en la vida,
> Sin cosa propia, fe ni gloria,
> Entre gentes ajenas
> Y sobre ajeno suelo
> Cuyo polvo no es el de mi cuerpo;
> No con el pensamiento vuelto a lo pasado,
> Ni con la fiebre ilusa del futuro,
> Sino con el sosiego casi triste
> De quien mira a lo lejos, de camino,
> Las tapias que de niño le guardaran
> Dorarse al sol caído de la tarde,
> A ti, Escorial, me vuelvo.

The earlier comparison of Castile to a *regazo* is now fully complemented and defined by an equally familial one of the Escorial as the mute protector of the child. But as is often the case with this poet, he explores all possible implications, and details even further this personification of the Escorial. The quest for protection and permanence is a rejection of all that is inessential and mutable. For Cernuda, who so often has been rashly accused of "hedonism," it brings with it a revulsion at the idea of love, since it constricts the self, prevents man from fulfilling his own personal destiny within the designs of Fate.

Hay quienes aman los cuerpos
Y aquellos que las almas aman.
Hay también los enamorados de las sombras
Como poder y gloria. O quienes aman
Sólo a sí mismos...
    ... ...
    ... Pero en la vida todo
Huye cuando el amor quiere fijarlo.
Así también mi tierra la he perdido,
Y si hoy hablo de ti es buscando recuerdos
En el trágico ocio del poeta.

The full meaning of the edifice should not be construed as mere nostalgia in the mind of an exile; by a carefully developed argument which manipulates the physical characteristics of the Escorial into a spiritual reality in the poet's mind, it becomes the symbol of a transcendent faith:

Tus muros no los veo
Con estos ojos míos,
Ni mis manos los tocan.
Están aquí, dentro de mí, tan claros
Que con su luz borran la sombra
Nórdica donde estoy...

Cernuda's technique of restoring reality through remembrance is achieved by contrasting opposite physical characteristics. Let us examine them; the initial set of opposites wes contained in the fruit:

O fruto de granada, recio afuera,
Mas propicio y jugoso en lo escondido.

This comparison of the inner and outer characteristics of the fruit, and by analogy the monastery itself, was then extended to a "vertical" set of opposites:

Si hacia los cielos anchos te alzas duro,
Sobre el agua serena del estanque
Hecho gracia sonríes...

Throughout the poem there are a series of expressed opposites' which reflect Cernuda's intention of viewing the Escorial as a summation of Christian man, the arbiter in the conflict between the soul and the body.

Eres alegre, con gozo mesurado
Hecho de impulso y de recogimiento,
Que no comprende el hombre si no ha sido
Hermano de tus nubes y tus piedras.
Vivo estás como el aire
Abierto de montaña,
Como el verdor desnudo
De solitarias cimas,
Como los hombres vivos
Que te hicieron un día,
Alzando en ti la imagen
De la alegría humana,
Dura porque no pase,
Muda porque es un sueño.

Here the conflict it between "dureza" and "alegría." Ortega y Gasset's essay on the Escorial employs a similar terminology: "... en este monumento de nuestros mayores se muestra petrificada un alma toda voluntad, todo esfuerzo, mas exenta de ideas y de sensibilidad. Esta arquitectura es toda querer, ansia, ímpetu". [1] However, the philosopher and the poet come to different conclusions — Cernuda sees repose and quiescence along with the "ímpetu." For the poet, the Escorial is a unique combination of will and belief, the spirit made stone.

Agua esculpida eres,
Música helada en piedra.

In the poem "Atardecer en la catedral," which is analyzed later in this chapter, the cathedral receives the same kind of epithet:

Como un sueño de piedra, de música callada, ...
La catedral extática aparece...

The contradictory aspects of Cernuda's vision are aggravated by his realization of the uselessness and futility of the edifice. It is the result of the desire of man who wishes a refuge for his spirit. Its impracticality has a great attraction for Cernuda; he envisions beauty as just that which serves no real function, a superfluous

---

[1] José Ortega y Gasset, "Meditación del Escorial," in *Obras completas* (Madrid, 1957), II, p. 557.

thing. In many ways, the Escorial and Spain remain a refuge for the spirit of the poet condemned to exile, even though this consolation is effected only through memory. For Cernuda, the Escorial is

> El himno de los hombres
> Que no supieron cosas útiles
> Y despreciaron cosas prácticas.
> ... ...
> Junto a una sola hoja de hierba,
> ¿Qué vale el horrible mundo práctico
> Y útil, pesadilla del norte,
> Vómito de la niebla y el fastidio?
> Lo hermoso es lo que pasa
> Negándose a servir...

The monastery is the product of a mind and a country that are faithful to themselves and their ideals, thereby incurring the disdain of more "practical" societies, and in turn ending by bringing financial ruin upon their own country. The solitude of the Escorial and its architect-king, the solitude of Spain among nations is thus analogous to the fate of useless and unessential beauty in the face of reality. The Escorial, like the figure of the poet, celebrates the world of the spirit by its single-minded alienation from the practical world. The "trágico ocio del poeta" is renewed again, the repose of the Escorial and that of the poet now function together. The observer and the observed are one. The strophe which describes the monastery in this regard could just as easily refer to the poet.

> Tú conoces las horas
> Largas del ocio dulce,
> Pasadas en vivir de cara al cielo
> Cantando el mundo bello, obra divina,
> Con voz que nadie oye
> Ni busca aplauso humano, ...

The personification is total, for all the qualities that Cernuda sees in the Escorial are refracted images of himself as poet. The fidelity to the self that he advocates is equally viable for the edifice:

> ... su sino quiere
> Que cante, porque su amor le impulsa...

The oppositions continue, but now they are concentrated in a musical image which transcends and recapitulates the previously stated formulae:

> Así te canto ahora, porque eres
> Alegre, con trágica alegría
> Titánica de piedras que enlaza la armonía(.)

The fusion of the Escorial and the poet is repeated again, for all flux is resolved into peace and harmony, all dichotomies resolved. Here the building serves as a means which brings about the serenity of the viewer. Its harmony resolves all conflict through the healing power of faith. The serenity that the poet imputes to the Escorial is one that derives from a changeless and immutable belief. The coalescence of man and stone has the profoundest motivation — man, desiring immortality, unifies himself with the stone in order to live beyond his measure. In these final lines, Cernuda wishfully strives to attain a union with the inanimate.

> Y si el tiempo nos lleva, ahogando tanto afán insatisfecho,
> Es sólo como un sueño;
> Que ha de vivir tu voluntad de piedra,
> Ha de vivir, y nosotros contigo.
>
> (*RD.*, pp. 179-182.)

The two qualities which seem to affect Cernuda most keenly in these meditations are the repose and solitude of the edifices. Both aspects coincide, and not fortuitously, with the poet's own view of his own role. The repose of the Escorial finds its own echo in the *trágico ocio* of Cernuda himself, and the solitude of the monastery's surroundings mirrors the alienated state of exile in which the poet finds himself. In his poem "Atardecer en la catedral," Cernuda envisions the cathedral with the same mixture of fervent adoration and identification, the same images of filial warmth and piety reappearing in a somewhat altered fashion. The physical description of the cathedral is executed in almost the same terms as those of the Escorial.

> Como un sueño de piedra, de música callada,
> Desde la flecha erguida de la torre
> Hasta la lonja de anchas losas grises,
> La catedral extática aparece,
> Todo reposo: vidrio, madera, bronce,
> Fervor puro a la sombra de los siglos.

Cernuda's idea of architectural construction encompassing all contradiction reappears. The cathedral defies time, for it converts fervor and faith into permanence. It is a living testament to a totally intangible spiritual impulse. Since *sombra* is almost always used by Cernuda to represent death, he means to show the fact that the religious faith which was the impulse that fired the original builders has remained pristine throughout the centuries. Just as the Escorial offered harmony to the observer, the cathedral brings an analogous sense of peace to the visitor.

> Aquí encuentran la paz los hombres vivos,
> Paz de los odios, paz de los amores,
> Olvido dulce y largo, donde el cuerpo
> Fatigado se baña en las tinieblas.

The peace that Cernuda senses is akin to that experienced by the child at home. The Escorial called forth a similar feeling of protectiveness and warmth: "... con el sosiego casi triste / De quien mira a lo lejos, de camino, / Las tapias que de niño le guardaran." This father-son relationship between the poet and the edifice is carried even further in this poem:

> Como el niño descansa, porque cree
> En la fuerza prudente de su padre;
> Con el vivir callado de las cosas
> Sobre el haz inmutable de la tierra,
> Transcurren estas horas en el templo.

As was the case with Cernuda's vision of the Escorial, the cathedral contains a harmony and peace which elevate life to another realm.

> No hay lucha ni temor, no hay pena ni deseo.
> Todo queda aceptado hasta la muerte
> Y olvidado tras de la muerte, contemplando,
> Libres del cuerpo, y adorando,
> Necesidad del alma exenta de deleite.

It is only within this peace and repose that the poet can ever have any sense of the Divine. Indeed, the references to the Divinity which end this poem are perhaps some of the most suggestive for a study of the religious impulse in Cernuda. The pronounced atheism and nihilism which he professed in the prose statement which prefaced a selection of his poems in the Gerardo Diego anthology has now, under the effect of the Spanish Civil War and exile in England, altered to a great degree; the poet admits to a vague sense of the Divine while contemplating the cathedral:

> Llanto escondido moja el alma,
> Sintiendo la presencia de un poder misterioso
> Que el consuelo creara para el hombre,
> Sombra divina hablando en el silencio.

However, the silence or the harmony which the poet perceives within the cathedral hardly has a lugubrious connotation. On the contrary, it affirms life, just as the quiescence of the tree contained the fullness of life:

> Aromas, brotes vivos surgen,
> Afirmando la vida, tal savia de la tierra
> Que irrumpe en milagrosas formas verdes,
> Secreto entre los muros de este templo,
> El soplo animador de nuestro mundo
> Pasa y orea la noche de los hombres.
>
> (*RD.*, pp. 153-155.)

In the poem "Ruiseñor sobre la piedra" we witnessed an identification or metamorphosis of the poet into stone — the palace and cathedral have a massive calm about them which affects the poet deeply. This attraction to serenity is not only a characteristic of these poems — speaking now of the two poems on the subject of cemeteries, it is not difficult to find the same structure as that of the previous poems, the same kind of utilization of reality. The first, "Cementerio en la ciudad" expresses Cernuda's bitter revulsion toward the city and a corresponding pity for the dead buried in it.

The structure of the poem is based upon an initial enumeration of what is seen, and then developed into a subjective commentary on the description. In the words of a perceptive commentator of this poem, "... el punto de partida natural está en la descripción del cementerio ciudadano, y sólo de ahí se pasa a la imagen principal, a través de la identificación, por proyección, de los sentimientos del sujeto lírico con las presuntas sensaciones que todavía experimentarán los "huesos viejos (v. 15) dentro de la tumba... la primera estrofa (vv. 1-7) no contiene una sola palabra que no tenga un valor inmediato de descripción objetiva." [2]

> Tras de la reja abierta entre los muros,
> La tierra negra sin árboles ni hierba,
> Con bancos de madera donde allá a la tarde
> Se sientan silenciosos unos viejos.
> En torno están las casas, cerca hay tiendas,
> Calles por las que juegan niños, y los trenes
> Pasan al lado de las tumbas. Es un barrio pobre.

This cemetery is not at all a resting place. It does not represent the eternal sleep of the just. It is continually hounded by the passing trains, just as the dead are aroused by the Channel guns in the Thomas Hardy poem which is the antecedent of Cernuda's — "Channel Firing." [3] The comparison between the two poems carried out by Juan Ferraté tells us how the cemetery is used as a symbol of protest against the encroaching civilization which

---

[2] Juan Ferraté, *La operación de leer* (Barcelona, 1962), pp. 230-231.
[3] I reproduce here only the first strophe:

> That night your great guns, unawares,
> Shook all our coffins as we lay,
> And broke the chancel window-squares,
> We thought it was the Judgement-day
> And sat upright ...

Thomas Hardy, "Lyrics and Reveries" in *Satires of Circumstance* (London, 1914), p. 7.

threatens both the living and the dead. Placed as it is in the midst of the city, it is no longer capable of having any religious inference; quite the contrary, the materialism that the city embodies for Cernuda has afforded him an appropriate focus for an atheistic vision of life. This is intensified by the realization that the cemetery is a displaced object within the city, a mute sign of the forgotten dead among so much heedless life.

The second strophe begins a gradual process of identification and sympathy with the nameless people buried beneath. The increasing warmth and human empathy on the part of the poet are apparent, in spite of the still evident tendency toward objectivization:

> Como remiendos de las fachadas grises,
> Cuelgan en las ventanas trapos húmedos de lluvia.
> Borradas están ya las inscripciones
> De las losas con muertos de dos siglos,
> Sin amigos que les olviden, muertos
> Clandestinos. Mas cuando el sol despierta,
> Porque el sol brilla algunos días hacia junio,
> En lo hondo algo deben sentir los huesos viejos.

The colloquial tone of the last line is an indication of the poet's own increasing interest and sympathy in their fate — "...ya plenamente expresiva de la identificación sentimental del sujeto hablante con el objeto de su contemplación..." [4] The dead do not enjoy an eternal silence and rest. Instead, life intrudes rudely:

> Ni una hoja ni un pájaro. La piedra nada más. La tierra.
> ¿Es el infierno así? Hay dolor sin olvido,
> Con ruido y miseria, frío largo y sin esperanza.
> Aquí no existe el sueño silencioso
> De la muerte, que todavía la vida
> Se agita entre estas tumbas, como una prostituta
> Prosigue su negocio bajo la noche inmóvil.

In the poet's imagination, the racket of the city corresponds to the trumpets of the Last Judgment awaited by the true believer. There is a similar confusion in the Hardy poem where the dead,

---

4 Ferraté, *La operación,* p. 231.

hearing the guns, mistake the throbbing for fanfares announcing the day of judgment and so their freedom from the grave. "We thought it was Judgment Day / And sat upright." The dead in Cernuda's poem are tricked in the same way.

> Cuando la sombra cae desde el cielo nublado
> Y el humo de las fábricas se aquieta
> En polvo gris, vienen de la taberna voces,
> Y luego un tren que pasa
> Agita largos ecos como bronce iracundo.
> No es el juicio aún, muertos anónimos.
> Sosegaos, dormid; dormid si es que podéis.
> Acaso Dios también se olvida de vosotros.
>
> (*RD.*, pp. 165-166.)

The sounds that reach the dead are not those of Gabriel's trumpets; in reality they are nothing but voices from a pub and the roar of a passing train. However, they sound to the dead like the announcement of Judgment Day. The deception is bound to be repeated daily until the end of the world. The liberation of that day, both feared and desired, is not about to come, and the only hope for the dead is a forgetfulness of an absent-minded Divinity. If they have been forgotten by God, they will escape the implacable judgment by reason of their own anonymity and oblivion in the eyes of God, a few dead among so many.

A similar poem from a much later collection, "Otro Cementerio" from the book *Vivir sin estar viviendo* is so analogous in tone and usage to the previous poem that the reader can only suppose that its inspiration came from a rereading of the earlier work. The brute objectivity in the description is tempered somewhat by a more traditional vision of the graveyard:

> Tras de la iglesia, en este campo santo
> Que jardín es y es camino,
> A cuyas losas grises
> Árboles velan y circunda hierba,
> El sol de mediodía, entre dos nubes,
> Desciende para el hombre vivo o muerto.

As was the case in the poem "Cementerio en la ciudad," there is a clear suggestion of a divine indifference toward men in the symbolism afforded by the warmth of the sun's rays. However, this function is counteracted by the trees and the grass which guard the stones in a protective or paternal manner. The cemetery is seen as a haven, much in the same way as the Escorial, which was personified as a *regazo* in the poem "Ruiseñor sobre la piedra." The disturbing, almost apocalyptic vision of the city in the previous poem here gives way to a more contemplative view of the cemetery and the forgotten dead.

> Remanso te aparece verde y sosegado,
> No lugar que se evita, mas retiro
> Donde acudan los vivos a sentarse,
> Igual que tú, como descanso en las tareas;
> Donde jueguen los niños, con costumbre
> Del paraje final en nuestra muerte...

> (*RD*., p. 254.)

The old men who take their leisure in the cemetery are a prefiguration of the fate of all humanity. The children, unconscious of the import or the meaning of the place, playfully make use of it just as they would any other. There is a kind of respect and confidence in the actions of both men and children; this is understandable enough, but are the dead able to forgive God's forgetfulness as easily?

The cemetery represents for Cernuda the effective symbol of the oblivion that is the fate of numberless dead; whether in the city or not, the noise of the trains and the brawling from the pubs, the careless play of children on the tombstones, all sum up their fate. The impotence of the dead is total, they cannot protest. They have no effect on life, so to speak, and thus the symbolism of the cemetery is bound to be passive, for the actual evidences of life lived in the past are only the memorial tablets. These do not afford the poet a range of implications that might bring the dead back to life again through poetry. In the search for a theme that would convey more cogently an increasing preoccupation with death and time, Cernuda amplifies the concept or his poems concerning the Escorial, the cathedral and the cemetery by making use of a topic that recapitulates all of these — ancient ruins. At the outset, Cernuda eschews the nocturnal and macabre aspect of ruins that so fascinated European Romantics: the "picturesque" qualities inherent in the theme are of no interest to the poet. The sheer evocative power that the sight of ruins can bring forth out of a sensitive poet is to be seen in one of the great antecedents of Cernuda's poems: "A las ruinas de Itálica," by Rodrigo Caro. There is more than a fortuitous coincidence of topic, since both poets approach the ruins with the same attitude. Also, the language employed by Cernuda has its basis in the earlier poem of Caro. In any case, the topic is more capable of sustaining a meditation on death, for the evidences of life destroyed surround the poet.

The vividness with which Caro calls forth the wreckage of the past is made all the more moving with the actual naming of the objects seen:

> ... Sólo quedan memorias funerales
> donde erraron ya sombras de alto ejemplo;
> este llano fué plaza, allí fué templo;
> de todo apenas quedan las señales;
> del gimnasio y las termas regaladas
> leves vuelan cenizas desdichadas ...

Both poets begin with an evocation of the silence, solitude and peace of the ruins, but Caro's *desengaño* is directed to the person of Fabio:

> Estos, Fabio, ay dolor! que ves ahora
> Campos de soledad, mustio collado
> fueron un tiempo Itálica famosa; ... [5]

Cernuda, on the other hand, using a typical opening of his late non-dramatic style, forsakes the projected poetic voice and reverts instead to an inner monologue:

> Silencio y soledad nutren la hierba
> Creciendo oscura y fuerte entre ruinas,
> Mientras la golondrina con grito enajenado
> Va por el aire vasto, y bajo el viento
> Las hojas en las ramas tiemblan vagas
> Como al roce de cuerpos invisibles.

---

[5] Rodrigo Caro, "A las ruinas de Itálica," in *The Oxford Book of Spanish Verse* (Oxford, 1945), pp. 209-210.

Cernuda tends to compare architecture to music, following Goethe, since he envisions man's drive to construct as yet another proof of his thirst for harmony and concordance in life. For Cernuda, a great edifice is music in which the stones are the notes of the whole symphony. We recall that the cathedral was termed "un sueño de piedra, de música callada," the Escorial as "agua esculpida" and "música helada." Here the same musical analogy is used, but this time the observer's own imagination (sueño) must complete the edifice, for it lies in ruins:

> Puro, de plata nebulosa, ya levanta
> El agudo creciente de la luna
> Vertiendo por el campo paz amiga,
> Y en esta luz incierta las ruinas de mármol
> Son construcciones bellas, musicales,
> Que el sueño completó.

From his contemplation, the poet can only derive one conclusion: this is man's fate. Before the levelling force of time upon the grandiose buildings, the poet can only protest.

> Esto es el hombre. Mira
> La avenida de tumbas y cipreses, y las calles
> Llevando al corazón de la gran plaza
> Abierta a un horizonte de colinas:
> Todo está igual, aunque una sombra sea
> De lo que fue hace siglos, mas sin gente.

Time is an invincible element for Cernuda. It is best to recognize its power over us, he maintains, for only this realization can impel us to savor the experience of living more acutely. The sacred character of the monuments, both extant and in ruins, is cherished by him, for he senses in them a higher permanence. The ruins, it is true, are shattered stone, but they still give signs of life, they are still victorious over time. Their beauty, then, exists outside of time, and it is to these broken but triumphant stones that the poet directs his meditation.

The water flowing through the aqueduct is an example of the non-temporality of the ruins: "pasa con la enigmática elocuencia / De su hermosura que venció a la muerte." What gives the place its special eloquence in Cernuda's mind, just as it did for Caro, is the *evidence* that it possesses of life's having been lived centuries ago. In describing what he sees, Cernuda begins with the mausoleums, but quickly leaves these memorials of the dead and turns to real indications of life: from the "tumbas vacías, las urnas sin cenizas," he goes to "las piedras que los pies vivos rozaron / En centurias atrás..." and "las columnas / En la plaza, testigos de las luchas políticas, / Y los altares donde sacrificaron y esperaron, / Y los muros que el placer de los cuerpos recataban." One sees how much more fruitful are the ruins to Cernuda's purpose than the mute cemetery: the vanity of life is more vivid and evident to him.

The final paradox lies in the fact that man is able to create beauty and permanence in stone, but is unable to retain mastery over what he has wrought. His creation is *almost* timeless; the creator himself has, like the fruit that was used as a symbol in "Ruiseñor sobre la piedra," an inner core of death. This does not extend to the things that he has created around him:

> Mas los hombres, hechos de esa materia fragmentaria
> Con que se nutre el tiempo, aunque sean
> Aptos para crear lo que resiste al tiempo,
> Ellos en cuya mente lo eterno se concibe,
> Como en el fruto el hueso encierran muerte.

There is a further paradox whose implications are explored in the next strophe. If time, death and the resultant thirst for eternity are the outer boundaries of man's existence, why were they infused into man, and what was the reason for this consciousness of eternity without the means to achieve it? This idea has sprung from the poet's contemplation of the ruins; before him are the stones, columnns and altars whose very existence are testimony of the imperfect ability of beauty to outlast time. These are nothing in comparison to the poet's ambition, for he not only wants to be eternal, but he demands to be alive at the same time. It is this ambition, spurred on by the poet's retrospection on the ruins, that forces him to question the motivations of God, His impassivity before so much destruction:

> Oh Dios. Tú que nos has hecho
> Para morir, ¿por qué nos infundiste

> La sed de eternidad, que hace al poeta?
> ¿Puedes dejar así, siglo tras siglo,
> Caer como vilanos que deshace un soplo
> Los hijos de la luz en la tiniebla avara?

Instead of deriving a Christian abhorrence of the world and its
vanity, undergoing a religious illumination that might give him
the necessary armor to defend himself against the world, Cernuda
denies the very existence of the Deity and thereby implies the
same lesson as the Stoics: the mutability of things should not
impel us to despise the world, but just the contrary:

> Todo lo que es hermoso tiene su instante, y pasa.
> Importa como eterno gozar de nuestro instante.
> Yo no te envidio, Dios; déjame a solas
> Con mis obras humanas que no duran: ...

If we are to enjoy life at every instant with no thought of an
afterlife, we imply that there are no ultra-terrestrial punishments
or rewards. Even if there are, Cernuda insists that they are not
worth the having. God is the product of fear, therefore non-
existent. "Mas tú no existes. Eres tan sólo el nombre / Que da el
hombre a su miedo y su impotencia..." With no expectation or
hope of eternity, the poet has only one recourse for his life on
earth, and that is a vain attempt to effect a metamorphosis of the
mutable into the immutable. For this reason, life is all the more
tantalizing, for it unfolds surrounded by death. Even within the
realm of life itself, the effect of time upon man foreshadows his
own death. "¿Es menos bella (la vida) acaso / Porque crezca y
se abra en brazos de la muerte?"

All this has come about through Cernuda's particularly personal
kind of stoicism as directed to the puzzle of the ultimate meaning of the ruins. Cernuda envisions his subject in the broadest
sense possible in order to extract from it its ultimate philosophical
implications. In this particular case, the topic is imbued with
analogies and applications that can easily be surmised by the
utilization of the meditative technique. The classic elegies have
had an effect upon the poet; he exhorts himself to *learn* from his
contemplation. "Aprende, pues, y cesa de perseguir eternos dioses
sordos." Consequent to the expression of this didactic purpose,

the strophe ending the poem returns to the self-address with which the poem began:

Sagrada y misteriosa cae la noche,
Dulce como una mano amiga que acaricia,
Y en su pecho, donde tal ahora yo, otros un día
Descansaron la frente, me reclino
A contemplar sereno el campo y las ruinas.

(*RD.*, pp. 187-189.)

It is a common trait of Cernuda to repeat in a later book the topic of a poem treated earlier. Thus we have "Otro cementerio" from *Vivir sin estar viviendo*, deriving from the earlier "El cementerio" from the previous book, *Como quien espera el alba*. In the same way the poem "Otros tulipanes amarillos" from the same book has an antecedent in the poem "Por unos tulipanes amarillos" from "Invocaciones." But "Otras ruinas," from *Vivir sin estar viviendo*, does not have a precedent in the poem "Las ruinas" just discussed. It is dissimilar because it takes as its topic not the ruins caused by the simple effects of time, but rather the havoc wrought by Hitler upon a defenseless country: the poet contemplates the ruins of London after an air raid by the Luftwaffe. The intention of the poem can only be the reverse of that of "Las ruinas." The change in focus brought about by the Spanish Civil War and the subsequent World War was to leave the imprint of historical forces upon Cernuda's thematics. In the previous poem on ruins, the only destructive force at work was that of time itself. This alone induced a state of crisis in the poet which eventually confirmed his view of the inevitability of time's processes: the only attitude to take before it was one of total resignation. But no one could expect the poet to retain this passive submission before Time in the face of a completely man-made force whose only ideal was frenetic and disordered action. In the poem "Otras ruinas," the central theme is no longer the workings of Time upon man's achievements, but rather a strongly felt criticism of the mechanistic civilization that is responsible for the ruins that the poet has before him. However, this sentiment is not just a protest *contra las máquinas*: the poet's concern goes deeper. He discards any aesthetic objections that might be made about contemporary industrial civilization. Instead, he centers his argument on the gradual impoversihment of the ethical ideal under the stress of materialism and *Realpolitik*. Because our civilization has been constructed by the machine, it is only logical, Cernuda maintains, to expect an equally mechanical and inhuman force to arise in the event of armed conflict:

> La torre que con máquinas ellos edificaron,
> Por obra de las máquinas conoce la ruina,
> Tras de su ordenación quedando a descubierto
> Fuerzas instigadoras de torpes invenciones: ...

The absurdity and disorder of the war finds its final symbol in the staircase of a shattered tenement which leads to nothing: "...tramo de escaleras que conduce a la nada / Donde sus moradores irrumpieron con gesto estupefacto, / En juego del azar, *sin coherencia de destino.* " (Italics mine) The coherence, which Cernuda saw so clearly in the fate of the Roman ruins, is a simple acceptance of the world; this acceptance should not be considered as a comprehension or an understanding of it, but rather a description of how it seemed to the poet. The workings of Fate are not to be questioned. They are unknowable but they *are* coherent, for the ruins represent the natural wearing away of all things due to time and the encroachments of Nature. The devastation of London, however, is not this at all: it is an unnatural and mechanical destruction which enrages the poet, since it does not reflect the world as changed by time, but rather by the machinations of avarice. The coherence found in the contemplation of Itálica encounters its antithesis in the unordered play of chance. "Intacto nada queda, aunque parezca / Firme, como esas otras casas hoy vacías." Going even further, Cernuda defines the motivation behind man's machines and their ability to arouse the destructive rage in humans; essentially, the poet finds that the root lies in the Faustian paradox of man armed well enough with the tools of his intellect, but without the guide of faith or morality that would orient his efforts toward a goal. "... Aquella / Que con saber sin fe quiso mover montañas; / Toda ella monstruosa masa insuficiente:..." Man, representing and guiding this destructive force, can only die at the hands of his own creation, for he and the city that is about to be destroyed again are one:

El hombre y la ciudad se corresponden
Como al durmiente el sueño, al pecador la trasgresión oculta;
Ella y él recusaron al silencio de las cosas
Hasta el refugio último: el aire inviolado,
De donde aves maléficas precipitaron muerte
Sobre la grey culpable, hacinada, indefensa,
Pues quien vivir a solas ya no sabe, morir a solas ya no debe.
Del dios al hombre es don postrero la ruina.

(*RD.*, pp. 249-251.)

No matter whether the object chosen for the meditation be animate or inanimate, whether it be Nature, a flower, a tree, the Escorial, the cathedral or a ruin, Cernuda's final aim has been an escape from the self, an estrangement of his spirit from his body so that the former might live on through the resultant union with the object observed. It is of no import that this ambition cannot be realized — it is the desire of man to avoid death that we all recognize immediately. Given the finite condition of man, the goal could not be but hopeless and unattainable.

The poet's desire takes the form of a projection of the self into the object seen. At times it is manifested in a desire for physical union, at times a passive and complacent identification with the object, similar to the protectiveness and total assurance experienced with the Escorial and the cathedral. The escape from the self can take other avenues and techniques: in the case of the late poetry of Cernuda, there is an increasing preoccupation with the creation of different voices, distinct dramatic characters and roles which extend the poet's self into selves which are not the poet's. In many cases there is a fluctuation in the distance maintained between the created figure and its creator, the more objective ones offering greater opportunity for satire and allegorization.

V

THE PROJECTED VOICE

Cernuda is a revealing example in contemporary Spanish letters of a poet who has consistently demanded that artistic creation be independent of inordinate *expression*. The poet, like Yeats and Eliot, achieves a distance between himself and his poetry through the creation of another poetic voice, a perspective upon the self which can impassively observe it; this projection serves as another focal point which, like a magnet, attracts the poet's mind away from a concentration on his own image. Clearly, there must be a fluctuation in degrees of distance; some of the "voices" or "characters" which the poet creates are autonomous in themselves and bear no resemblance to him; others contain clearly recognizable subjective elements that bring the figure closer to the creator. These projections afford the poet a role considerably different from his own, a consciousness which is not his, but still created by him. "No brute animal can act a role. Unable to recognize himself, he finds it impossible to recognize what by contrast with self is other. By the same token, he has nothing against which to set a role so that it is a role." [1]

In this attempt to be what he is not, the poet exteriorizes himself in another in order to avoid sentimental communication, merely personal expression of the self. The classic form is *persona*, "that through which the person speaks." "The symbol of the exteriority of a literary creation is the mask, for in such a creation

---

[1] Fr. Walter J. Ong, "Voice as Summons for Belief," in *The Barbarian Within* (New York, 1962), p. 54.

the author does not communicate directly, but through a kind of covering or disguise, fictitious persons or characters, who are more or less in evidence and who speak his words." [2]

The manipulation of poetic voices in Cernuda's late poetry reflects his impulse to go beyond the self, to create "others" through which he might view his own being. The consciousness of his own solitude among men brings an examination of the self by these projected characters. The *desdoblamiento* is Cernuda's unique means of doing this. Speaking of the later poetry, a Cuban critic notes "...un desdoblamiento del yo poético, que permite al discurso lírico surgir como un monólogo o, si se quiere, como un diálogo dramático. La forma más sencilla o elemental será la del uso de una segunda persona, de un tú, que apuntaría a la única alteridad posible, por ahora, de un poeta que canta desde los posos más hondos de su soledad." [3] The fact that the late poetry of Cernuda often takes the form of dialogue, be it self-address or a projected voice of another dramatic character, is a reflection of the poet's increasing didacticism. The dialogue form is a useful medium for philosophical discussion and "differences of opinion." We cannot imagine, for instance, the infinite varieties of opinions and ideas in a Platonic dialogue being expressed by Plato alone. Each character forcefully takes up his own line of argument, and from the dramatic conflict that ensues between these clashes, a kind of synthesis appears in the mind of the reader that closely approximates, but never defines, the actual truth of the matter. In Cernuda's case, he ranges from a simple "yo" to a gradual projection into another voice which does not resemble the personal one. The distance between the lyric and the dramatic is not only concerned with the burden of ideas in poetry. The creation of another character is dramatic and theatrical, for it asks the poet to *be* the image in the mirror, totally outside of himself. In this way, he may candidly see himself impersonally. No one has understood the dangers of lyricism better than Yeats, greatly admired by Cernuda. Yeats's achievement is the creation of the mythical "other" that is distinct from the self. "There is a relation between discipline and the theatrical sense. If we cannot imagine

---

[2] *Ibid.*, p. 53.
[3] José Olivio Jiménez, *Cinco Poetas del Tiempo* (Madrid, 1964), p. 120.

ourselves as different from what we are and assume that second self, we cannot impose a discipline upon ourselves, though we may accept one from others. Active virtue as distinguished from the passive acceptance of a current code is therefore theatrical, consciously dramatic, the wearing of a mask." [4] The expression of the self becomes for both Cernuda and Yeats the anti-ideal, that which must be avoided. "Personal utterance is beset always by the danger of sentimentality which leads poetry away from that reality the poetry would deal with to various kinds of self-pity and self-deception. (Yeats's) problem, therefore, was to discover a technique by which the personal could somehow be objectified, be given the appearance of impersonal "truth" and yet retain the emotive force of privately felt belief." [5] In Yeats's case, this objectivity and distance was partly gained by the use of the mask. The more generic term would be *persona*, which puts the poet's own personal voice a full degree away from his own self by placing the responsibility for the words uttered on another character, another self. This creation of the mythical is the highest degree of self-consciousness; it entails the formation of another who will direct and observe the creator. "The lyric is or becomes dramatic when it presents not a single point of view but a struggle between conflicting points of view. The deliberate placing of a distance between the poet and his lyric person effectively dramatizes the substance of the poem." [6]

One could immediately protest: are the *personae* or the masks evasions or obfuscations of the self rather than revelations of more significant aspects of reality? This is not the case: on the contrary, the use of *personae* in the late poetry more effectively conveys the contradictions which the poet embodies. These divergences within the self are better rendered by dramatic characters, just as the differences among humans are better conveyed by Plato's cast of characters than would be the case if he were to present various anecdotes and opinions of those same characters within a philosophical treatise that had Plato

---

[4]   W. B. Yeats, *Autobiography* (New York, 1938), pp. 400-401.

[5]   John Unterecker, "Faces and False Faces," in *Yeats, A Collection of Critical Essays* (Englewood Cliffs, 1963), p. 30.

[6]   George T. Wright, *The Poet in the Poem* (Berkeley, 1960), p. 7.

alone as the "narrator." Thus the *personae* do not obscure the poet.
On the contrary, they often "reflect the complexity, the contradictions, the intricate inconsistencies we know to be characteristic of
human beings, reflect them in compressed and economical form." [7]
This objectivity is strangely pleasing to Yeats: "I take pleasure
alone in those verses where it seems to me I have found something
hard and cold, some articulation of the Image, which is the opposite of all that I am in my daily life, and all that my country
is." [8]

Many of Cernuda's *personae*, especially that of Philip the
Second in such a poem as "Silla del rey," will speak a language
of Calderonian majesty and grandeur. Each *persona* demands his
own voice, each one demands adjustment of the poetic word to
conform to the psychological demands of the character. In English

---

[7] *Ibid.,* p. 22.

[8] Unterecker, *Yeats, A Collection,* pp. 31-32. The use of the word
"image" by Yeats is indicative of the Platonic background in his own poetry
and that of such similar sprits as T. S. Eliot and Cernuda. The classic text
for the definition of representation through *personae* occurs in the third
book of *The Republic:*

> "You know the beginning of the *Iliad,* where the poet says that
> Chryses begs Agamemnon to release his daughter; and when
> Agamemnon gets angry and refuses, Chryses calls down the wrath
> of the gods on the Greeks?" "Yes."
> "Well, up to the words 'He appealed to the whole Achaean army,
> and most of all to its two commanders, the sons of Atreus,' the
> poet is speaking in his own person and does not attempt to persuade
> us that the speaker is anyone but himself. But afterwards he
> speaks in the person of Chryses, and does his best to make us think
> that it is not Homer but an aged priest who is talking . . . And when
> he speaks in the person of someone else, may we not say that he is
> imitating as nearly as he can the manner of speech of the character
> concerned?"

Plato, of course, dissaproves of this technique; it is for him illusory shadow-
boxing on the part of painters and poets. For Cernuda, Yeats, T. S. Eliot,
Browning et. al., it constitutes the essence of greatness in poetry; the *mimesis*
is the means by which the subjective is suppressed, and therein true grandeur.
Plato goes much farther in Book Ten, where he extends the argument to
comprehend artistic creation as a whole, this matter best exemplified by the
controversy concerning the essential form of a bed (God's) and such secondary
and tertiary phenomena made or represented by a carpenter and a painter
respectively. As the title of Cernuda's collected poetry indicates, all of this
is of immense importance to the philosophical concept behind *La realidad
y el deseo.*

literature, Browning must be recognized as the consummate master of "dramatic poetry." Speaking of Browning's characters, George Wright states that "not only do his *personae* customarily use the tones of ordinary talk, but they are not heroes, only protagonists, and their virtues are considerably qualified by their faults." [9]

The projection of the voice which Cernuda admires and adapts as his own is above all a basis for the creation of a private mythology, evoking through poetry the appearance of objective truth. It might be supposed that this effort of the poet to give his verses an objective character through the use of such religious characters as Lazarus, or historical ones as Philip the Second, might have a distracting effect upon the reader who is ostensibly in search of the original self of the poet. Contrary to expectations, our attraction to the poetry grows in exact proportion to the distance between the subjective self of the poet and the poem: "insofar as the work is objectified, set apart from the existent writer who gives it being ... its evocative effect becomes more poignant: ... as the masklike detachment grows, the evocative quality of the work, its pull on the sensibility of the reader, grows. [10] A poem thus advertises the distance and remoteness, which, paradoxically, are part of every human attempt to communicate." [11] The "distance and remoteness" of which Father Ong speaks is exactly analogous to the "something hard and cold" which Yeats found in his best verses.

There remains one problem: the function of the reader in this kind of poetry. Before, the reader could expect an intimate confidence between the poet and himself, where the relation was that of "I" to "you"; he now experiences a kind of estrangement when reading a poet such as Cernuda, since the reader no longer plays an organic role in the poem. The poet is not interested any longer in forming an emotional "bond" with the reader — exactly the opposite, he wishes to project himself into other selves and beings. The reader must reorient himself away from the personal and subjective utterance to a mythic and objective one. As Father

9   Wright, *The Poet in the Poem,* p. 48.
10   Ong, *The Barbarian Within,* p. 59.
11   *Ibid.,* p. 62.

Ong has pointed out, this too has its own kind of hold upon the reader, but not until he has accustomed himself to a new kind of subjectivity, where the self is not presented in the poem directly. The reader no longer participates, he observes or overhears. "The poet takes it upon himself to challenge the gods on man's behalf and in so doing creates his own vocation. But to speak *for* man is not at all the same as speaking *to* man, and in fact, Cernuda's poems are rarely addressed to the reader at all but to himself or a counter-self, such as his demon; or else they take the form of dramatic monologues wherein the reader has no part at all inasmuch as the dramatic monologue creates its own listener. The reader of Cernuda's poems does not hear but rather overhears." [12]

There are different degrees of objectivity in any *persona*, just as there are differing usages of the poetic voice. We are interested in the voice that is most distant from the person of the poet — the third voice. T. S. Eliot has given us the classic definition: "the first voice is the voice of the poet talking to himself — or to nobody. The second is the voice of the poet addressing an audience, whether large or small. The third is the voice of the poet when he attempts to create a dramatic character speaking in verse; when he is saying, not what he would say in his own person, but only what he can say within the limits of one imaginary character addressing another imaginary character" [13] Cernuda's late poetry demands a slight variation of the preceding; the poet addresses an imaginary character not for dramatic effect alone, but so that the imaginary character might speak back to him.

The first examples of this dramatic poetry of dialogue are found in *Las nubes*, reflecting his new readings and outlook as an exile in England. His interest in the projection of the poetic voice was initiated by a reading of Robert Browning, a master at creating a character in verse, an example of the "third voice." Speaking of Browning's discursive and colloquial style, Cernuda finds that in many cases "...En su poesía ... muchos de los temas responden a creencias que rigen la conducta del hombre, siendo frecuente que exponga puntos de vista diferentes en torno a una

---

[12] Silver, A Study, p. 177.
[13] T. S. Eliot, "The Three Voices of Poetry" in *On Poetry and Poets* (London, 1957), p. 89.

situación o problema humano, sin decidir entre ellos, como ocurre en "The Ring and the Book," "Bishop Bloughram's Apology" o "Mr. Sludge, 'The Medium.'" [14] Cernuda's definition of Browning's poetry is peculiarly applicable to his own late poetry. Speaking of Browning again, he characterizes the poetry as "...poesía dramática; es decir, fluctuación y ajuste incesante de la palabra para trazar con ella los movimientos del pensamiento y de la pasión en la hondura del ser humano." [15] Cernuda's interest in dramatic techniques is not evidenced by an abrupt appearance of various "voices" in the poetry. There is a tentative attempt in the poem "La fuente," then a broader range of various points of view in the dramatic poem "Resaca en Sansueña," and fully developed in the darkly pessimistic *auto* entitled "La adoración de los Magos," where the three kings represent three attitudes of pessimism or belief before the appearance of the star in the East.

It is peculiarly fitting that, in this stage of Cernuda's discovery of the myriad voices of poetry, we should begin with an analysis of "La fuente." The poet, contemplating the fountain in the Luxembourg Gardens in Paris, finds in the stone and water a perfect image for his own poetry.

The poet no longer speaks — rather he speaks as if he were the voice of the fountain. "Poetry, symbolized by the upward thrust of water from a fountain, delivers a soliloquy." [16] The voice of the poet in the first person no longer speaks, but rather the projection of the self into the founntain so that it expresses itself with the poet functioning as an artificer of the ideas that are then symbolized and enacted, as it were, by the voice of the fountain.

The reader has no indication that anyone else but the poet himself is speaking, but references to the jet of water directed to the sky and to the moss at the base of the fountain should be sufficient indication that a substantial alteration of focus has taken place:

---

[14]   Luis Cernuda commenting on his own translation of Browning's "A Toccata of Galuppi" in *Poesía y literatura*, p. 111.

[15]   *Ibid.*

[16]   Silver, *A Study*, p. 179.

Hacia el pálido aire se yergue mi deseo
Fresco rumor insomne en fondo de verdura,
Como esbelta columna, mas truncada su gracia
Corona de las aguas la calma ya celeste.

Cernuda's observation of the objects of the world, whether animate or inanimate, always begins with a fidelity to selective physical characteristics. Then, he fits these details into a new metaphysical relation. In the third strophe of the poem the fountain affirms that the precipitous existence of the water that is sent skyward, pausing for a microsecond in perfect equilibrium between the initial thrust and the gravitational force that will bring it to earth again, is an exact physical correlation of our own life to the infinite number of years that have passed an are about to come. The effusion of water, its momentary halting in the air, are compared to the flow of time and the transient nature of our lives within it. But the poet goes even further, for he ascribes to the voice of the fountain a third relation, that of the water and the stone. The stone is not modelled haphazardly: it is a motionless and permanent embodiment of one of the numberless "moments" in the "life" of the water. Thus the stone represents mutability and flux, for it is essentially a single instant that is frozen into eternity. "The fountain arrests each moment, confounds death and is thus the perfect embodiment of the poet's credo. Protean, melodious and insubstantial, it yet endures as it aspires." [17]

Al pie de las estatuas por el tiempo vencidas,
Mientras copio su piedra, cuyo encanto ha fijado
Mi trémulo esculpir de líquidos momentos,
Única entre las cosas, muero y renazco siempre.

Previously, in the poems "Ruiseñor sobre la piedra" and "Atardecer en la catedral," stone always represented being in movement, flowing. In the former poem, the walls of stone were described as "agua esculpida... música helada en piedra." The cathedral as "fervor puro a la sombra de los siglos." In each case, the stone still contains the initial impulse of the architect and the builder.

---

[17] *Ibid.*

Just as the Escorial and the cathedral contain innumerable blocks of stone which in themselves are nothing, just as the water contains countless atoms which in themselves, without relation, are not water, the endless flow is an image of life itself, for it reflects all of experience, yet is calm and ordered:

> Este brotar contínuo viene de la remota
> Cima donde cayeron dioses, de los siglos
> Pasados, con un dejo de paz, hasta la vida
> Que dora vagamente mi azul ímpetu helado,
>
> Por mí yerran al viento apaciguados dejos
> De las viejas pasiones, glorias, duelos de antaño,
> Y son, bajo la sombra naciente de la tarde,
> Misterios junto al vano rumor de los efímeros.

The conclusion of the poem stands as a concentrated summation of Cernuda's *ars poetica*. Poetry's unique source of gratification to man derives from the sound of the endlessly flowing water — its unordered potential plays a melody which gives an other-worldly contentment to the hearer:

> El hechizo del agua detiene los instantes:
> Soy divino rescate a la pena del hombre,
> Forma de lo que huye de la luz a la sombra,
> Confusión de la muerte resuelta en melodía.
>
> (*RD.*, pp. 143-144.)

The consequences of this projection of the voice into another figure are of great relevance to the later development of the poetry. When the poet says "soy," we now experience a double perspective, for the poet, after all, has written the poem, but the actual voice is the inanimate stone, so that we view the poet's image of himself and his poetry as refracted through this "other," the fountain. What had to be avoided here was a "confession" which would have had more to do with the person of Luis Cernuda than with his poetry. The latter is never a by-product of the emotions of the poet; Cernuda's "pudor" is a constant throughout his work. In transferring his voice to the fountain, he has found the perfect vehicle to divorce the poet from the poem and thereby create a distance between the creator, the work of art, and the audience which views, hears or reads it.

The three-part poem "Resaca en Sansueña," which carries the significant title of "Fragmentos de un poema dramático," marks a further advance in this technique. The section which is of special interest at this point is solely the second of the three that the poet consented to publish. The last line of the prologue, that is to say, the first section, indicates the dramatic and theatrical character of the ensuing monologue: "comienza el drama ahora. Escuchad silenciosos." The statue's speech is another attempt by the poet to project himself, but in contrast to "La fuente," the speech of the statue resembles to a great extent that of the poet speaking in the first person. There is almost a total identity between the projected voice and the poet's own, but nevertheless it forms the basis for a subsequent broadening of the poet's ability to create alien characters which will culminate in the long poems concerning Philip the Second.

After a preliminary introductory strophe, the poem resolutely begins in the first person, the statue speaking:

> Uno a uno los siglos morosos del destierro
> Pasaron sobre mí. Soy la piedra divina
> Que un desastre arrojara desde el templo al abismo,
> Poniendo al poderío término entre las sombras.

The situation reminds us of the placement of the statues of antiquity in museums and gardens of cities, exiled from their own Attic surroundings. Just as was the case with the figures in "A las estatuas de los dioses," their divinity comes from the symbolic intent of the statues, a representation of youth and beauty.

> Soy aquel que remotas edades adoraron
> Como forma del día. Mancebos y doncellas
> Con voces armoniosas elevaban al aire
> Himnos ante la gloria blanca de mis columnas.
>
> Pero los pueblos mueren y sus templos perecen,
> Vacíos con el tiempo el cielo y el infierno
> Igual que las ruinas. Vinieron nuevos dioses
> A poblar el afán temeroso del hombre, ...

The alteration of the structure of belief, the transition from paganism to Christianity, has left the statues without a sacred function in the contemporary world. As was the case with the Escorial and the cathedral, the stone still retains the impulse that brought it into being, and the remembrance of this brings with it an irrepressible sense of melancholy, for even the stone that is the statue is gradually corroding and losing its obliviousness to time:

> Lleno estoy de recuerdos. Su tormento me abre
> Como llaga incurable el hueco de la gloria,
> Gloria que no soñé, gloria que yo llevaba
> Con su nimbo visible de luz sobre mi frente.
>
> Pasan mientras las olas con revuelta marea
> A juntar con sus aguas las aguas del olvido,
> Y recubren mi cuerpo, blanco como las nubes,
> Del limo que corroe los mármoles sagrados.

Although the statue's physical and spiritual exile seems complete, it still aspires to return to earth:

> Aún espero el rescate de las aguas profundas,
> La paz de las auroras futuras, devolviendo
> A la tierra algún día este mármol caído,
> Forma mortal de un dios inerme entre los hombres.
>
> (RD., pp. 151-152.)

Cernuda's definition of dramatic poetry, "... fluctuación y ajuste incesante de la palabra para trazar con ella los movimientos del pensamiento y de la pasión en la hondura del ser humano," [18] is not yet applicable to the poetry read so far. As readers, we have experienced a poetic voice other than that of the poet, but there is still no conflict of different voices which dialogue among themselves around a theme. The creation of myriad voices does not occur until the end of the book Las nubes, specifically the dramatic poem "La adoración de los Magos." It is true that the poem Lázaro appears in Las nubes between the "Resaca en Sansueña" and "La adoración de los Magos;" this poem will

---

[18] Cernuda, Poesía y literatura, p. 111.

be analyzed in the chapter describing the different *personae* of Cernuda. Thus "La fuente" and "Resaca en Sansueña" are preliminary efforts toward the goal of dramatic poetry, while "La adoración de los Magos" and "Noche del hombre y su demonio" are fully dramatic interplays among different voices, representing Cernuda's own solution to the problem of dramatic poetry. The poem "Lázaro" will be analyzed in the next chapter, dedicated to the poems of historic and legendary characters.

However, "Lázaro," "La adoración de los Magos" and the other *personae* of Cernuda are intimately related to each other in that they are allegories relating to the self of the poet. Some of the figures assimilate a biographical situation; such is the case with "Lázaro," a work which is indubitably related to a sense of rebirth felt by Cernuda during the first few years of exile in England. Others, such as the Magi or Philip the Second, are more autonomous personages, existing at a considerable distance from the poet. To a greater or lesser extent, these figures are all allegories, since they do not exist for themselves within the poem, but rather are adapted, detail for detail, to the expressive necessity of the poet. In this sense, they are only forms whose content is supplied by Cernuda. In the particular case of "La adoración de los Magos," each of the kings represents only *one* of the poet's many and changing attitudes toward belief, each one nonetheless being a part of the whole that is the poet's spiritual condition.

The legend of the Magi attracted Cernuda for good reason: in giving a different philosophical and religious orientation to each one of the kings, he has divided the conflicts within himself and given them roles. The source of the legend is to be found in Matthew, II, 1-12. Cernuda, an avid reader of the King James version while in England, was familiar with this and the attendant tradition describing their physical characteristics and the significance of each one of the kings' gifts. The legend is striking for the implications of cowardice and disbelief in the kings, and this has been mirrored in Cernuda's somber poem. The physical characteristics of the wise men, which Cernuda will faithfully follow in his poem, have been ascribed to the Venerable Bede. Bede regarded them as representing the thre continents of Europe, Asia and Africa; hence the medieval and modern portrayals of them as belonging to the white, brown and black race, respectively. Melchor is the oldest of the three, Gaspar the young and fair-haired, while Baltasar is the Negro with a thick beard. Melchor brings the frankincense; Gaspar, the gold; Baltasar, the myrrh, used for embalming in ancient times, and thus a prefiguration of Christ's fate on earth. Cernuda has based the divergence of philosophical ad religious outlook of each upon an imaginative elaboration of the implications that he himself drew from the kings' physical characteristics. There still remains one obvious source, however — El auto de los reyes magos. Certainly, this is the closest to the spirit of Cernuda's poem, for the underlying element of doubt and disenchantment found in it are also a part of Cernuda's work. Indeed, the element of skepticism in the medieval auto is exactly the point of contrast between it and the orthodox interpretation found in Matthew. Speaking of the auto, Wickersham Crawford notes that "the play opens with three monologues amounting to fifty-one lines, in which the author adds some original features in his description of the Wise Kings by telling of their doubts as to whether the new star in the heavens really betokens the Saviour's birth..." [19] Thus the patent doubt of Melchor and Baltasar surely must derive from the same kind of disconcerting skepticism that the kings show before the star of the east in the Auto de los reyes magos. [20]

In this poem, Cernuda will present and inspect three antagonistic philosophical positions. For the first time in the poetry of Cernuda, we experience wholly created poetic voices or masks that disagree among themselves as to the import and the meaning of what they have seen, thus conforming to the idea of various presentations of divergent points of view around a single topic: in a word, poesía dramática. In his effort to objectify experience

---

[19] J. P. Wickersham Crawford, Spanish Drama before Lope de Vega (Philadelphia, 1937), pp. 1-2.

[20] In passing, mention should be made of the Libro dels treis reys d'orient, which is orthodox in its interpretation of the kings. However, T. S. Eliot's "The Journey of the Magi" (1927) presents the kings as believers in the divinity of the child, but their spiritual disquiet commences when they realize that the old beliefs that reign in their respective kingdoms have been destroyed by the birth of Christ.

through poetry, Cernuda created truly dramatic characters. The various philosophical viewpoints found in this contemporary *auto* are really a kind of impassive examination of the whole spectrum of faith from blind belief to worldly skepticism. [21]

The work is divided into five parts, the first entitled "Vigilia"; it presents Melchor, the old man, speaking a soliloquy which is a meditation on what is about to come. The second part, "Los reyes," presents the different kings in fully elaborated monologues which are in effect extended discourses on the ultimate ramifications of each king's attitude toward the star and the Christ child. The third part, "Palinodia de la esperanza divina," is, as one might expect from the title, the most profoundly pessimistic section, spoken by an unnamed voice speaking for the three kings. The importance of this anonymous voice is discussed fully below; Cernuda wished to create a voice that was one of the kings, but none of them in particular. Having already established their divergent interpretations of the star, the poet assigned to this summation a narrative voice that might be interpreted as being that of any one of the three. The fourth part, "Sobre el tiempo pasado," presents an anonymous shepherd, who further complicates the interaction of the different roles by his modest and unassuming description of the kings as they passed by his flock on the way from Bethlehem. The perspectivism is enhanced by the fact that the shepherd is speaking from a point in time well after the fact, so that the whole history of the kings, including their return to their homelands, is recounted by him. The fifth and final section, "Epitafio," is a kind of moral drawn by the poet himself.

Melchor's speech, which occupies all but two lines of the first section, "Vigilia," places the reader outside the realm of the poem so that he is able to observe the effect of the star upon the desolation and melancholy of the old man. Cernuda puts

---

[21] There is a striking similarity in form between this poem and Yeats's short drama *The Resurrection*. In this work, written for the Abbey Theatre in 1934, three characters who are identified only by their nationalities discuss from their own particular point of view the meaning of the event. They are, in order of appearance, "The Greek, The Hebrew and The Syrian." I have no doubt that Cernuda was familiar with this work; he was, after all, an ardent Yeatsian.

a special emphasis upon the gradual physical collapse of the old king, later contrasting with the newly found energies and hopes that the star awakens in him:

> La soledad. La noche. La terraza.
> La luna silenciosa en las columnas.
> Junto al vino y las frutas, mi cansancio.
> Todo lo cansa el tiempo, hasta la dicha,
> Perdido su sabor, después amarga,
> Y hoy sólo encuentro en los demás mentira,
> Aquí en mi pecho aburrimiento y miedo.
> Si la leyenda mágica se hiciera
> Realidad algún día.

Still within his own kingdom, the psychological state of the king is established quite graphically. The "leyenda mágica" of the Saviour-to-be-born is consequently the last hope of the old man. Even though the legend is a sacred one for Melchor, he doubts that he will live to experience it. The king has suffered so much disillusionment and illusory hope that he fears the star may well be nothing but a celestial phenomenon unrelated to the coming of Christ. "Así al tiempo sin fondo arroja el hombre / Consuelos ilusorios, penas ciertas, / Y así alienta el deseo." The desire for a consummated and justified life, one that is not at all interrupted or broken by death, is Melchor's final wish, thus making death simply another link in the great chain of being. "Señor, danos la paz de los deseos / Satisfechos, de las vidas cumplidas. / Ser tal la flor que nace y luego abierta / Respira en paz." But the star does appear, and with it, the sleep of centuries in which men have languished for so long comes to an end. Melchor's speech ends with a supplication to God that his death be postponed so that he might see the Redeemer incarnate.

> Hombres que duermen
> Y de un sueño de siglos Dios despierta.
> Que enciendan las hogueras en los montes,
> Llevando el fuego rápido la nueva
> A las lindes de reinos tributarios.
> Al alba he de partir. Y que la muerte
> No me ciegue, mi Dios, sin contemplarte.

The second section opens with the speech of Baltasar, who gives us the first indication of the melancholic pessimism which characterizes the kings' reaction to the appearance of the star in the east. He compares the kings to nomadic shepherds, following a weak and ill-defined star:

> Como pastores nómadas, cuando hiere la espada del invierno,
> Tras una estrella incierta vamos, atravesando de noche los
> [desiertos,
> Acampados de día junto al muro de alguna ciudad muerta,
> Donde aúllan chacales; ...

In contrast to Melchor's transcendent belief in the salvation of man through grace, Baltasar has nothing but disdain for the search for transcendent truth. According to him, man should not spend his life seeking out the secret of the universe, but should accept the domestic virtues as the end of his quest; anything more would be the act of demented men. Baltasar is essentially in the tradition of the Stoic humanist, whereas Melchor is a prophet in his own country determined to view the realization on earth of what he envisions. Attacking the search for truth, Baltasar preaches a reorientation of man's life so that it is fulfilled on this earth, with no ultra-terrestrial punishments or rewards:

> Buscamos la verdad, aunque verdades en abstracto son cosa
> [innecesaria,
> Lujo de soñadores, cuando bastan menudas verdades acordadas.
> ... ...
> No se hizo el profeta para el mundo, sino el dúctil sofista
> Que toma el mundo como va: guerras, esclavitudes, cárceles y
> [verdugos
> Son cosas naturales, y la verdad es sueño, menos que sueño
> [humo.

The last line, which is essentially a reversal of the terms of one of the sonnets of Quevedo, presents the transcendent truth as a dream, and the world as the only reality, whereas for Quevedo and Calderón, the opposite was true.

Baltasar's complaint against the search for an illusory truth is based upon a stoic contentment with the order of the world as found. Gaspar, on the other hand, accepts Baltasar's contempt for transcendent truth, but places this rejection on a different basis — a hedonism and glorification of sexual satisfaction as the only fruitful aspiration for man. The symbols are the garden, the home, the young wife awaiting the return of her husband:

> Amo el jardín, cuando abren las flores serenas del otoño,
> El rumor de los árboles, cuya cima dora la luz toda reposo,
> ... ...
> Cuando la noche llega, y desde el río un viento frío corre
> Sobre la piel desnuda, llama la casa al hombre,
> ... ...
> Un cuerpo virgen junto al lecho aguarda desnudo, temeroso,
> Los brazos del amante, cuando a la madrugada penetra y duele
> [el gozo.
> Esto es la vida. ¿Qué importan la verdad o el poder junto a esto?
> Vivo estoy. Dejadme así pasar el tiempo en embeleso.

With two of the three monologues completed in this second section, it is evident that Cernuda has projected two entirely dissimilar figures into the *personae* of the Magi: one, Baltasar, personifies the wholehearted acceptance of the lies of the world in place of the Truth. The other, Gaspar, is content to remain at home with his wife, just like the invited guest in the Gospels who turns down the invitation at the last minute because he is too occupied with his new bride to attend the banquet .

The third speech in this section is given by Melchor, who, in language of Calderonian grandeur, rejects the specious reasoning of the other kings and attempts to redirect them to the transcendent message of the star. The basic theme is uttered in the first line, "No hay poder sino en Dios, en Dios sólo perdura la delicia," which reminds the worldly kings of the transitory nature of power and love, insisting again that these things are to be found only in God:

> El mar fuerte es su brazo, la luz alegre su sonrisa.
> Dejad que el ambicioso con sus torres alzadas oscurezca la
> [tierra;
> Pasto serán del huracán, con polvo y sombra confundiéndolas.
> Dejad que el lujurioso bese y muerda, espasmo tras espasmo,
> Allá en lo hondo siente la indiferencia virgen de los huesos
> [castrados.

¿Por qué os doléis, oh reyes, del poder y la dicha que atrás
[quedan?
Aunque mi vida es vieja no vive en el pasado, sino espera;
Espera los momentos más dulces, cuando al alma regale
La gracia, y el cuerpo sea al fin risueño, hermoso e ignorante.

The believer that is Melchor lives in the future through hope, but the pagan desperately lives through memory and nostalgia of pleasures and things that decay and pass away. Melchor insists that the hope of truth implied by the star is the only bedrock upon which man can construct his life. "Abandonad el oro y los perfumes, que el oro pesa y los aromas aniquilan. / Adonde brilla desnuda la verdad nada se necesita." The dialogue between the three kings now becomes more acrimonious, for the conflict breaks out into the open, with mutual accusations and scorn. Baltasar is the first to object, with a cruel attack upon the Biblical rhetoric so convincingly employed by Melchor:

Antífona elocuente, retórica profética de raza a quien escapa
[con el poder la vida.
Pero mi pueblo es joven, es fuerte, y diferente del tuyo israelita.

Gaspar, with his accustomed indifference to History and God, insists upon conserving his hedonistic delight in the mutable.

Si el beso y si la rosa codicio, indiferente hacia los dioses todos,
Es porque beso y rosa pasan. Son más dulces los efímeros gozos.

Melchor, in his final speech in this second section, demands again that they follow his path. His unique weapon in this vain attempt to convince the others is, however, an irrational one. He threatens them with his own armies:

Locos enamorados de las sombras ¿Olvidáis, tributarios
Cómo son vuestros reinos del mío, que aún puedo sujetaros
A seguir entre siervos descalzos el rumbo de mi estrella?
¿Qué es soberbia o lujuria ante el miedo, el gran pecado, la
[fuerza de la tierra?

The third section, "Palinodia de la esperanza divina," presents an unusual technical problem, since this narration of the meeting of the three kings with the Christ child and their ultimate disillusionment is recounted in the first person plural. In the previous speeches, each one of the kings has vigorously asserted his own identity through the disparity among themselves. Now the voice is in no way recognizable as one of the three, yet since the narration is in the first person plural, there is no choice but to consider it a voice that speaks for all without being any one in particular.

It would not be surprising to find that Gaspar and Baltasar were unable to believe in the divinity of the Christ child, but Melchor's loss of faith is no less complete. The narrator is explicit on this point: "... pero ninguno / De nosotros su fe viva mantuvo."

The "Palinodia" begins with a description of the wasted and barren countryside that the kings pass through as they travel to Bethlehem, a desolation that is a kind of premonition of the arid life without faith that they are about to live:

> Era aquel que cruzábamos, camino
> Abandonado entre arenales,
> Con una higuera seca, un pozo, y el asilo
> De una choza desierta bajo el frío.
> ... ...
> Padecíamos hambre, gran fatiga.
> Al lado de la choza hallamos una viña
> Donde un racimo quedaba todavía,
> Seco, que ni los pájaros lo habían
> Querido. Nosotros lo tomamos:
> De polvo y agrio vino el paladar teñía.
> Era bueno el descanso, pero
> En quietud la indiferencia del paisaje aísla,
> Y añoramos la marcha, la fiebre de la ida.

Finally arriving at the destination indicated by the star, the kings enter the stable and find not the Divinity, but only a child of itinerant nomads:

> Hallamos una vida como la nuestra humana,
> Gritando lastimosa, con ojos que miraban
> Dolientes, bajo el peso de su alma
> Sometida al destino de las almas,
> Cosecha que la muerte ha de segarla.

Part of their disillusionment stems from the idea within their imaginations concerning the physical appearance of God on earth: "Esperamos un dios, una presencia / Radiante e imperiosa." What they saw did not correspond to what they had imagined, and they are disenchanted. Confiding their thirst for faith in men and the world, they leave determined to live "sin adorar a dios alguno," all transcendent faith destroyed:

> Nuestros dones, aromas delicados y metales puros,
> Dejamos sobre el polvo, tal si la ofrenda rica
> Pudiera hacer al dios. Pero ninguno
> De nosotros su fe viva mantuvo,
> Y la verdad buscada sin valor quedó toda,
> El mundo pobre fue, enfermo, oscuro.

This *auto* is very much that of a skeptic. Cernuda's kings are eminently men of the world whose inner desire for faith draws them to the star, but whose intellects rebel at bestowing divinity upon a simple child in a manger. The gifts are placed before the Christ child, but are only evidence of their shattered hopes. In the *Auto de los reyes magos,* the gifts were laid before the child as a test of his divinity, one of the unique heretical aspects of the work. The collapse of the kings' incipient faith was already foreshadowed by the bleak, uninviting surroundings and the bitter cold, but so too in the rancorous and complaining arguments of Gaspar and Baltasar. Nonetheless, Melchor's recantation is surprising. In the end, it must be seen as a final ironic fillip by the poet, who has carefully modelled Melchor's speeches on a Calderonian ideal of style and belief. The poet shows us that the archetypal figure from the age of faith could no more tolerate the actual sight of the carpenter's son in the manger than could the other more worldly kings. The speeches in Part Two which expressed so vividly and exactly the different world views of each king are now seen to be caustic portents of the collapse of belief and hope that the kings experience when they see the child who will be adored as the Divinity from that time on. "Ya al entrar en la choza descubrieron los reyes / La miseria del hombre, de que antes no sabían."

The fourth part, "Sobre el tiempo pasado," presents the reader with yet another perspective of the legend of the Magi, for here an aged shepherd recounts what he saw of the three kings when he was a young man. The shepherd's retrospective portrayal of the three kings passing by his flock is particularly moving:

> Tiempo atrás, siendo joven, divisé una mañana
> Cruzar por la llanura un extraño cortejo:
> Jinetes en camellos, cubiertos de ropajes
> Cenicientos, que daban un destello de oro.
>
> Venían de los montes, pasados los desiertos,
> De los reinos que lindan con el mar y las nieves,
> Por eso era su marcha cansada sobre el polvo
> Y en sus ojos dormía una pregunta triste.

Rather than confirming the divinity of the child, and wondering at the callousness of the kings in simply leaving their gifts and returning to their respective kingdoms without having found the hoped-for truth, the shepherd is in essential agreement with the kings: what they saw in the manger was not God, but the child of penniless nomads:

> Entonces fue refugio dulce entre los caminos
> De una mujer y un hombre sin hogar ni dineros:
> Un hijo blanco y débil les dio la madrugada.
> ... ...
>
> Luego, como quien huye, el regreso emprendieron.
> También los caminantes pasaron a otras tierras
> Con su niño en los brazos. Nada supe de ellos.
> Soles y lunas hubo. Joven fui. Viejo soy.

The apocryphal fate of the kings is elaborated by the shepherd:

> Gentes en el mercado hablaron de los reyes:
> Uno muerto al regreso, de su tierra distante;
> Otro, perdido el trono, esclavo fue, o mendigo;
> Otro a solas viviendo, presa de la tristeza.

The final strophe of this section is a summation of the import of what he has seen. In his disdain for history or religious belief, the shepherd approaches the attitude of the two young Magi:

Buscaban un dios nuevo, y dicen que le hallaron.
Yo apenas vi a los hombres; jamás he visto dioses.
¿Cómo ha de ver los dioses un pastor ignorante?
Mira el sol desangrado que se pone a lo lejos.

The shepherd asks us to contemplate the things of this world and disregard our impulse toward belief in a life beyond the present one.

Where is the voice of Cernuda in this poem? If we were to identify the thought of the poet himself as distinct from the other roles, it would probably be that of the ordinary man which the shepherd personifies. The final epitaph is yet another ironic twist by the poet; he affirms now that what the kings saw was the truth, but they were unable to recognize it as such:

La delicia, el poder, el pensamiento
Aquí descansan. Ya la fiebre es ida.
Buscaron la verdad, pero al hallarla
No creyeron en ella.

Ahora la muerte acuna sus deseos,
Saciándolos al fin. No compadezcas
Su sino, más feliz que el de los dioses
Sempiternos, arriba.

(*RD.*, pp. 167-175.)

Cernuda presents to us the human embodiments of divergent, not to say contradictory world views in the figures of the three Magi. Each one is distinct from the other; still all three project certain particular aspects of the poet's contradictory self. By going beyond himself through these "others," and then bringing about a conflict among them by use of dialogue, the poet has, in effect, dramatized himself. What is more, he has achieved a new objectivity in treating his own emotions and thoughts. A further disciplining of the emotions has been accomplished, banishing the excessive Narcissism of the earlier books; the examination of the self is not simply looking at the image in the pool. Instead, the poet projects different "portions" of his self into contrasting roles. These different points of view within the poet demand varying poetic voices; after they have spoken, a kind of *entente* is

reached. In the *auto* of Cernuda, the epilogue is given not by
any one of the kings, but by a voice which represents them all.

One could ask; is this not theater, after all, and not just a
projection of the voice of the poet? Such categorization here loses
its utility, for the dialogues and monologues that we have
examined have a theatrical quality to them, undoubtedly. It is
this element that Yeats advocated so strenuously: the poet can
discipline and order his thought only by means of dramatic
techniques in poetry. Cernuda has assumed many selves so that
his own may be defined more precisely.

The reader has little function in the poem. If anything he is
an irrelevant bystander who is the mere "recipient" of the poem,
without any of it being directly addressed to him. The drive
toward objectivity produces a fundamental estrangement between
the poet and the reader. The former's main concern is to inspect
his own condition through the medium of these roles. To this end
he creates other characters which aid him in carrying out this
self-examination. A diminution of expressed emotion is felt; a
philosophically-tinged language replaces that of a more subjective
poetry of the "first voice."

The other extended dialogue poem of Cernuda, "Noche del
hombre y su demonio," is not at all a religious poem. Instead,
the poet, through the medium of the devil, dialogues with himself
about the role of poetry in life, attempting at the same time to
justify his own gratuitous generosity in writing poetry to a callous
audience. Cernuda personifies the world's scorn of the poet by
making the devil represent the impulse that drives a poet. The
identification of the Devil with the poet's own conscience cannot
be accepted without some reservation, for it is actually just
another case of a projection by the poet into a contrary personality
so that he might examine his art more closely, but without the
moral overtones that the poet's conscience might demand of him.
Instead, Cernuda's devil is the *dämon* that Goethe cites as the
source of his poetic impulse, the fatal power which the poet
cannont resist. [22] No one has recognized the *dämon* within Cer-

---

[22]   Cernuda discusses the term and translates appropriate sections from
Eckermann's conversations with Goethe to illustrate it in the article "Palabras
antes de una lectura" in *Poesía y literatura,* p. 200.

nuda more acutely than his Mexican contemporary Octavio Paz:
"Cernuda ha sido fiel a sí mismo durante toda su vida y su libro,
que ha crecido lentamente como crecen los seres vivos, posee
una coherencia interior nada frecuente en la poesía moderna ...
Cernuda es uno de los raros poetas fatales. Escribe porque no
tiene más remedio que hacerlo ... un demonio, su implacable
conciencia poética, no lo suelta nunca y le exige, ocurra lo que
ocurra, que diga lo que tiene que decir." [23] The devil speaking
in "Noche del hombre y su demonio" is the same demon noted by
Paz in the poetic conscience of Cernuda.

The dialogue does not begin with an ordinary conflict between
the two characters. Instead, the poet is unconscious, asleep in a
state of reverie. The demon wakes him, insisting that he must
"cobrar tu señorío. / Percibe la existencia en dolor puro." The poet,
desirous of inner peace, and determined to throw off the implacable force dogging him, begs to be left alone. "Entre los
brazos de mi sueño estaba / Aprendiendo a morir. ¿Por qué me
acuerdas?" As the devil admits, he is a creation of man's
imagination, a kind of double created by man so that he can
see himself through the senses of another.

> No sólo forja el hombre a imagen propia
> Su Dios, aún más se le asemeja su demonio.
> ... ...
>
> En mí tienes espejo. Hoy no puedo volverte
> La juventud huraña que de ti ha desertado.

The Devil is not only the poet's poetic conscience, he is the
consciousness of time within him — the force that brings back
the pain of nostalgia and remembrance, impelling the poet to
eternalize the moment through poetry. The Devil now sets up a
set of opposites — art or life: "Ha sido la palabra tu enemigo:
/ Por ella de estar vivo te olvidaste." The poet cannot protest
at this, for any artist must sacrifice raw living in order to achieve;
but this is done in spite of an ever-increasing anguish as the
artist advances through life. The poet is the helpless servant of

---

[23] *Claridades Literarias* (May, 1959), p. 23.

the impulse that he senses within himself, and he regretfully
sacrifices his life to it:

> Hoy me reprochas el culto a la palabra.
> ¿Quién si no tú puso en mí esa locura?
> El amargo placer de transformar el gesto
> En són, sustituyendo el verbo al acto,
> Ha sido afán constante de mi vida.
> Y mi voz no escuchada, o apenas escuchada,
> Ha de sonar aún cuando yo muera,
> Sola, como el viento en los juncos sobre el agua.

The justification of the poet resides in the fact that he is able
to live beyond himself through the words that he has created, a
false eternalization of the self. The "sed de eternidad" is assuaged.
Obviously, this is only so if the poet is read and appreciated, and
the Devil makes this point rather acidly — given the fact that
few readers know that you exist now that you are alive, how
can you expect anything more during the years after your
death? The fate of poetry is put into question:

> Nadie escucha una voz, tú bien lo sabes.
> ¿Quién escuchó jamás la voz ajena
> Si es pura y está sola? El histrión elocuente,
> El hierofante vano miran crecer el corro
> Propicio a la mentira. Ellos viven, prosperan;
> Tú vegetas sin nadie.

The poet, describing all his doubts about his own usefulness and
function in society through another figure, has been able to achieve
an examination of conscience. The disdain of the devil goes to the
heart of the poet's questioning of himself:

> Me hieres en el centro más profundo,
> Pues conoces que el hombre no tolera
> Estar vivo sin más: como en un juego trágico
> Necesita apostar su vida en algo,
> Algo de que alza un ídolo, aunque con barro sea,
> Y antes que confesar su engaño quiere muerte.

Cernuda is here in dialectical opposition to the self. How else
could this be expressed than through dialogue, a form the poet
knew from his readings in the Classics and the dialogues of Gide

and Valéry? Speaking of one of Gide's dialogues, Cernuda notes that "... la tesis de Corydon se debate en forma de diálogo, forma que para un pensamiento como el de Gide, a veces en oposición dialéctica consigo mismo, resulta adecuada." [24] The opposing self is the last step in a process leading from the unexamined life to a heightened self-consciousness. The divisive self undergoes a split when the poet concedes to the devil that "me hieres en el centro más profundo." The solitude of the poet, the disdain of the world toward his work, his vain claim to superiority over other men by being the artist whose works exist after his death, all are shattered by the incisive *burla* employed by the devil. Here, he details all that the poet is not, but might wish to be.

> Siento esta noche nostalgia de otras vidas.
> Quisiera ser el hombre común de alma letárgica
> Que extrae de la moneda beneficio,
> Deja semilla en la mujer legítima,
> Sumisión cosechando con la prole,
> Por pública opinión ordena su conciencia
> Y espera en Dios, pues frecuentó su templo.

The same idea is expressed in Cernuda's commentary on *Corydon:* "No existe hombre, por inteligente y excepcional que sea, que no guste alguna vez de hallarse envuelto, al aprobar o desaprobar, con la masa del vulgo. Tal abdicación del juicio individual en favor del prejuicio colectivo tiene sus ventajas y hasta sus voluptuosidades." [25] Not at all a hard working member of the middle class, the poet, like Gide, always has that vigorous impulse toward the future and the unknown which set him apart from the rest. Happiness is not an ideal:

> ... ...
> Bien que no es la cuestión el ser dichoso.
> Amo el sabor amargo y puro de la vida,
> Este sentir por otros la conciencia
> Aletargada en ellos, con su remordimiento,
> Y aceptar los pecados que ellos mismos rechazan.

---

[24] "André Gide," in *Poesía y literatura*, p. 143.
[25] *Ibid.*, p. 144.

The devil, just as with Christ on the mountain top, suggests that the poet's ascetic and poverty-stricken existence is not worthy of him, and that he should act accordingly to change the situation:

> Pobre asceta irrisorio, confiesa cuánto halago
> Ofrecen el poder y la fortuna:
> Alas para cernerse al sol, negar la zona
> En sombra de la vida, gratificar deseos,
> Con dúctil amistad verse fortalecido,
> Comprarlo todo, ya que todo está en venta,
> Y contemplando la miseria extraña
> Hacer más delicado el placer propio.

The poet silences the Devil, and makes a definitive justification of his poverty and his alienation from society:

> ... ...
> Ahora silencio,
> Por si alguno pretende que me quejo: es más digno
> Sentirse vivo en medio de la angustia
> Que ignorar con los grandes de este mundo,
> Cerrados en su limbo tras las puertas de oro.

The Devil confesses his own defeat, and the personified opposite now agrees to a compromise between the poet and himself. The Devil willingly submits to the same fate as that of the poet:

> Después de todo, ¿quién dice que no sea
> Tu Dios, no su demonio, el que te habla?
> Amigo ya no tienes sino es éste
> Que te incita y despierta, padeciendo contigo.
> Mas mira cómo el alba a la ventana
> Te convoca a vivir sin ganas otro día.
> Pues el mundo no aprueba al desdichado,
> Recuerda la sonrisa y, como aquel que aguarda,
> Álzate y ve, aunque aquí nada esperes.
>
> (RD., pp. 221-225.)

From the simple projection of the self into another object or being in "La fuente" and the monologue of the statue in "Resaca en Sansueña," the poet has further developed his interest and skill in the use of dramatic effects that culminate in "La adoración de los Magos" and the dialogue "Noche del hombre y su demonio."

If Cernuda's stylistic and intellectual development were to end at this point, one could point to the achievement of dramatic poetry as the culmination of his attempt to attain a perspective upon himself through the medium of other characters. Each one of these characters has been adapted to the expressive needs of the poet, and their autonomy ranges from a barely concealed biographical situation that is allegorized to a completely elaborated character that has no subjective relation to the poet, thus being an objective inspection and expression of an alien point of view. But there are other personages — historical, religious or legendary characters such as Lazarus, Philip the Second, Caesar and an anonymous foot soldier who strongly resembles Bernal Díaz del Castillo. Through the alien ideas and language that the poet gives to these characters, he is able to achieve poetic satire.

VI

PERSONAE

Satire requires a knowing "edge" on the subject; there must be a certain calculation which will divorce the poet from the poem; in the various characters created by Cernuda in his late poetry, a base polemic is always avoided — he artfully adjusts his didactic ends to an artistic ideal by choosing a representative religious or historical personage which will willfully express all that is distant, even anathema, to the poet. The prejudices within Cernuda, his own spiritual stance, are conceptualized into the character so that we indirectly divine the thought of the poet. Thus these men —Philip the Second, Caesar, Lazarus, Bernal Díaz should not be seen as varying symbols for the poet, but rather allegories, for in symbol form and meaning are one, whereas an Allegory points to something other than its form— it is a mold to be filled by the poet-maker, and to be completed by the reader. [1]

The first poem, "Lázaro," is of special interest, for it is the least didactic of the four and consequently the most relevant to Cernuda himself. Concerning this poem, one of the few that the poet speaks of with some pride, Cernuda states that "... mientras Inglaterra y el mundo atravesaban la crisis que culminó en la visita de Chamberlain a Hitler, cierta calma melancólica fue invadiéndome, y apareciendo en los versos escritos entonces, después de la tormenta de la guerra civil. "Lázaro", una de mis composiciones preferidas, quiso expresar aquella sorpresa desen-

---

[1] See Fritz Strich, *Der Dichter und die Zeit* (Bern, 1947), pp. 21-22.

cantada, como si, tras de morir, volviese otra vez a la vida." [2]
As in "La adoración de los magos," a religious figure is created
by Cernuda in a peculiarly melancholic way. In this case, Lazarus is described as in a state of disenchantment, doubt, and
equivocation about the second life brought about by Christ's inter-
vention. [3] His doubt extends to the Maker: Christ is mentioned
only obliquely, and then as "él." Thus, "... él me había llama-
do / Y en mí no estaba ya sino seguirle."

The poem opens with a triple perspective on the event.
Although Lazarus is speaking, he recounts the circumstantial
details as they were told to him — "Así lo cuentan ellos que lo
vieron."

> Era de madrugada.
> Después de retirada la piedra con trabajo,
> Porque no la materia sino el tiempo
> Pesaba sobre ella,
> Oyeron una voz tranquila
> Llamándome, como un amigo llama
> Cuando atrás queda alguno
> Fatigado de la jornada y cae la sombra.

Alive again, he describes the experience of death, but with a
curiously ambivalet reaction to life begun anew. It is not another
life for him, but a repetition of the suffering that he thought he
had left behind:

> Era otra vez la vida.
> Cuando abrí los ojos
> Fue el alba pálida quien dijo
> La verdad...

Far from leaving the warmth of a mother, Lazarus leaves a
sepulchral womb. He senses the alienation from the world of one
who is living past his time. He does not want to return to life;
he wants only the sleep of the dead that he was just beginning to
experience. Christ's action may have been a miracle, but it is
an unwanted one:

---

2 Cernuda, *Poesía y literatura*, p. 260.
3 As recounted by John, XI: 1-44.

Quise cerrar los ojos,
Buscar la vasta sombra,
La tiniebla primaria
Que su venero esconde bajo el mundo
Lavando de vergüenzas la memoria.

Christ is just another Man of singular powers who, by his own spiritual generosity, brings Lazarus back to life. But the generosity is misapplied, he does not want to begin again. Nevertheless, Lazarus is still able to sense the compassion within the Man who wrought the miracle:

Entonces, hondos bajo una frente, vi unos ojos
Llenos de compasión, y hallé temblando un alma
Donde mi alma se copiaba inmensa,
Por el amor dueña del mundo.
... ...
Sentí de nuevo el sueño, la locura
Y el error de estar vivo,
Siendo carne doliente día a día...

The "disenchanted surprise" that Cernuda wishes to evoke in us through the person of Lazarus is analogous to the feelings of a human whose life has been spent, but who is forced to live another among the memories and surroundings of his earlier "incarnation."

... Puesto en pie, anduve silencioso,
Aunque todo para mí fuera extraño y vano,
Mientras pensaba: así debieron ellos,
Muerto yo, caminar llevándome a la tierra.
La casa estaba lejos;
Otra vez vi sus muros blancos ...

His own walk is that of a pallbearer, for he is carrying what was a corpse back into the realm of the living, a monstrous reversal of the funeral procession which accompanied him to the tomb four days before. This alienation from all that he knew continues; the grandeur of Christ's miracle is lowered to the level of a judicial sentence. Lazarus is *forced* to live. Cernuda implies that although Christ has given new physical life to Lazarus,

the soul which formerly inhabited the body has not been revivified
in the same way:

> Todos le rodearon en la mesa.
> Encontré el pan amargo, sin sabor las frutas.
> El agua sin frescor, los cuerpos sin deseo;
> La palabra hermandad sonaba falsa,
> Y de la imagen del amor quedaban
> Sólo recuerdos vagos bajo el viento.
> Él conocía que todo estaba muerto
> En mí, que yo era un muerto
> Andando entre los muertos.

The only hope of the dead man brought back to life lies in
Christ himself. He is the only recourse for Lazarus, who must
consciously bear all the trials of life without experiencing again
the innocence of childhood or the initial protection of the
family:

> Así pedí en silencio, como se pide
> A Dios, porque su nombre,
> Más vasto que los templos, los mares, las estrellas,
> Cabe en el desconsuelo del hombre que está solo,
> Fuerza para llevar la vida nuevamente.

The final strophe emphasizes the transient nature of this resurrection: Lazarus' life will not be renewed again on this earth,
but in Heaven. Thus the search for truth should be only and
uniquely a search for eternal life:

> ... ...
> Trabajando, no por mi vida ni mi espíritu,
> Mas por una verdad en aquellos ojos entrevista
> Ahora. La hermosura es paciencia.
> Sé que el lirio del campo,
> Tras de su humilde oscuridad en tantas noches
> Con larga espera bajo tierra,
> Del tallo verde erguido a la corola alba
> Irrumpe un día en gloria triunfante.
>
>   (RD., pp. 160-163.)

The sudden life of the flower is the new life of the spirit that
Lazarus longs for, distinct from the mere physical renewal that he
has just experienced.

This poem is particularly favored by the poet, for it represents a turning point in his constant effort throughout *Las nubes* to objectify and order his experience. If the biographical elements which form the basis of the poem are considered, the poet becomes a contemporary Lazarus: alone, having begun a new life in England, having escaped certain death in Spain. Like Lazarus, he has undergone a physical resurrection which demanded expression other than the personal, subjective evocation. The sentiments, thoughts, and emotions of the poet are dramatized and given much broader relevance to the reader by the use of a Biblical figure whose fortunes, as it were, are similar to the poet's own. In the poem, the poet has vanished behind his Biblical embodiment of life begun anew. If we insist on the importance of biographical details for an understanding of any poem, "Lázaro" might be cited, but certainly the reverse is not true. Lazarus is the particular mask which the poet found most expressive of a certain state of mind.

The allegorization reaches its final phase in three dramatic monologues: "Quetzalcóatl," whose subject is the conquest of the Aztecs by Cortés; "Silla del rey," where Philip the Second speaks as if seated on the stone throne placed on the mountainside for his use, where he could supervise the construction of the Escorial; "El César," whose subject is an aging emperor of the Roman Empire who is modelled on gleanings from Suetonius's *The Lives of the Caesars*. These three monologues are from historical personages who in themselves are alien to Cernuda, representing the most hateful aspects of civilization: Spain in America, the enigma of Spain, dictatorship. Here, the poet's mask is not an aspect of the divided self as in "Noche del hombre y su demonio," or a Biblical character representing the poet's condition as in "Lázaro," but antagonistic, autonomous personages who are in no way related to the poet's positive convictions except by inverse logic. We can discern Cernuda's vehement denunciation by means of the repugnant inhumanity and callousness of the characters that he has created.

In "Quetzalcóatl," we do not experience the emotions of the conqueror Cortés by his own narration, but rather by and unnamed soldier who could only be Bernal Díaz, for Cernuda makes some of Bernal's stylistic idiosyncracies his own. It would be appropriate to recall at this point that Quetzalcóatl was the semi-divine king of the Aztecs whose reincarnation on earth was expected in the same year that Cortés happened to land. [4] Because of this coincidence, Moctezuma welcomed the explorer as the personification of the god-king. One could infer a satiric twist to Cernuda's final intention in the poem, since the title points not to Bernal Díaz or to Cortés, but rather to the chance coincidence of the predictions of the astrologers and the landing of the explorers. In any case, Cernuda does not identify the narrator, and gives us only the minimum of details about him:

> No importa el nombre. Una aldea cualquiera
> Me vio nacer allá en el mundo viejo
> Y apenas vivo me adiestré en la vida
> Del miserable: hambre, frío, trabajo
> Con soledad. ¿Quién le dio al fango un alma?

This insistence on the anonymity of the speaker places us at yet another plane away from the events. The hardness of this soldier's early life is relieved by the incomparable Castilian sky that will later serve as a touchstone for his nostalgia:

> Pero tuve algo más: el cielo aquel, el cielo
> De la tarde en Castilla (puro y vasto
> Como frente de un dios que piensa el mundo,
> Un mar de sangre y oro, cuya fiebre
> La calmaba, toda azul, la noche honda
> Con su perenne escalofrío de estrellas) ...

The figure of Cortés is now introduced a man with singular bravery and courage who was destined to become more than other men:

> Pisando tierra nueva, de la mano el destino
> Me llevó llanamente al hombre designado
> Para la hazaña: aquel Cortés, demonio o ángel,

---

[4] "(Quetzalcóatl) promised, on his departure, to return at some future day with his posterity, and resume the possession of his empire ... A general feeling seems to have prevailed that the period for the return of the deity was near at hand." W. H. Prescott, *History of the Conquest of Mexico* (London, 1904), II, p. 10.

> Como queráis; para mí sólo un hombre
> Tal manda Dios, apasionado y duro,
> Temple de diamante, que es fuego congelado
> A cuya vista ciega quien le mira.

The expansion of the imagination before the limitless possibilities of the New World is perfectly conveyed by Cernuda, but the narrator's appetites are less worldly than those of his cohorts. The description of the humble soldier's eagerness only to *see* the marvels that have been described in legend is in sharp contrast to the other soldiers' ambitions:

> Y el momento llegó cuando nos fuimos
> Por el mar un puñado de hombres;
> El mundo era sin límite, igual a mi deseo.
> Frente al afán de ver, de ver con estos ojos
> Que ha de cegar la muerte, lo demás, ¿qué valía?
> Mas este pensamiento a nadie dije
> Entre mis compañeros, a quienes hostigaba
> La ambición de riqueza y poderío.

As Cernuda tells us later in the poem, the fantastic riches of the Aztec kingdom and the acquiescence of the natives soon turn the spectator that the soldier had hoped to be into an active participant in the pillage and destruction of the Indian civilization. The abrupt transformation of the would-be observer to the orgiastic plunderer is one of Cernuda's most telling strokes, for it is done without transition or evident motivation. The soldier follows the same rage to destroy that he had previously condemned in his companions. The deleterious effect of power on men is seen as an unleashing of the nihilistic impulse within every man:

> Astucia, fuerza, crueldad y crimen,
> Todo lo cometimos, y nos fue devuelto
> Con creces; mas vencimos, y nadie hizo otro tanto
> Antes, ni hará después: un puñado de hombres
> Que la codicia apenas guardó unidos
> Ganaron un imperio milenario.

The soldier immediately springs to his own defense: these actions are natural in time of war. Any act is permissible if it contributes to ultimate victory or to the soldier's contentment. Cernuda again emphasizes the effects of combat as the essential source of the moral decay of the soldier, who ostensibly began the expedition only to see and to marvel. But then again, the conquest had not begun:

> Ya sé lo que decís: el horror de la guerra,
> Mas lo decís en paz, y en guerra calláis con mansedumbre.
> Nadie supo la guerra tan bien como nosotros,
> Ni siquiera los hombres allá en el mundo viejo...

The theme of the poem is now clear — the barbarization of civilized man under the impulse of the thirst for power and riches in the New World. Not content with describing this precipitous abandonment of an ideal, the narrator details with evident pride the murder and pillage committed:

> Cuerpos acometí, arrancando sus almas
> Apenas fatigadas de la vida,
> Como el aire inconsciente las hojas de una rama;
> Destinos corté en flor, por la corola
> Aún intacto el color, puro el perfume.
> ¿Hubo algún Garcilaso que mi piedra
> Hundiera bruscamente al fondo de la muerte?
> El reino del poeta tampoco es de este mundo.

The conqueror thus is not content with the destruction of monuments and the slaughter of humans. His nihilism extends to art itself. The soldiers who were confused with gods act as arms of divine retribution. The final capitulation of Moctezuma is described with the same kind of overpowering "yoísmo" that is found in Bernal Díaz:

> Cuando en una mañana, por los arcos y puertas
> Que abrió la capital vencida ante nosotros,
> Onduló como serpiente de bronce y diamante
> Cortejo con litera trayendo al rey azteca,
> Me pareció romperse el velo mismo
> De los últimos cielos, desnuda ya la gloria.
> Sí, allí estuve, y lo vi; envidiadme vosotros.

The implied criticism of Cortés in the next strophe stems from the old soldier's distrust of regal courts and domesticity:

> Pero no es rey quien nace, y Cortés lo sabía.
> ¿Por qué lo olvidó luego, emulando con duques
> En la corte lejana, él, cuyos pies se hicieron
> Para besarlos príncipes y reyes?
> Cuando él se abandonó también Dios le abandona.

To confirm the perspective on the events just narrated, the poet reveals that the soldier is about to die, having outlived most of his fellow soldiers. The ideal of victors and vanquished now fades into a common fate undergone by all. Now the soldier wants only to know all this was done, in whose name, and to what end:

> Ahora amigos y enemigos están muertos
> Y yace en paz el polvo de unos y de otros,
> Menos yo: en mi existencia juntas sobreviven
> Victorias y derrotas que el recuerdo hizo amigas.
> ¿Quién venció a quién?, a veces me pregunto.

If the Aztecs were to suffer as they did, being the conquered, the conquerors suffered a no less drastic fate, for their spiritual decline coincided with the full exploitation of the riches of the New World. The land beheld by Bernal Díaz and Cortés as a realization of all their dreams has now been subjected to the demands slave trade and the "profit motive." Nothing remains of the pristine impulse to explore and to marvel that they sensed at first:

> Nada queda hoy que hacer, acotada la tierra
> Que ahora el traficante reclama como suya
> Negociando con cuerpos y con almas;
> Ya sólo puede el hombre hacer dinero o hijos.

In the end, all victories are pyrrhic: "oh tierra de la muerte, ¿dónde está tu victoria?"

(*RD,* pp. 208-212.)

"Quetzalcóatl" is one of the first of a kind of poem that will recur frequently in the late poetry of Cernuda; poetry of an objective and epic character. The use of the word "epic" should not be confusing; it only denotes the anonymous function of the poet in the poetry. The voice is still evident intermittently, but it is objectified in the "other" so as to make the person of Cernuda disappear into the projection. He now becomes the invisible poet who constructs dramatic characters that do not derive from his own sentiments or ideas, but rather those of the others he wishes to criticize. Obviously, there will always be a fluctuating degree of detachment or involvement with the mask or *persona*. In "Quetzalcóatl," there are many sentiments and ideas that happen to apply to Cernuda himself, for instance. In the two poems that will be analyzed in the remainder of the chapter, all subjective elements are banished in favor of complete objectivity. No intermediary is used to comment upon what has happened or to moralize on the events described.

Before discussing the poem "Silla del rey," it might be instructive to recall an earlier poem on the same subject, "Ruiseñor sobre la piedra." The basic ideas remain the same in both poems. The poet's spiritual image of the Escorial as a representation in stone of the soul of Spain is identically expressed in both, but the techniques employed to convey the thought are distinct. The earlier poem represented the voice of the exiled poet, speaking to the Escorial as he remembered it. The essence of the building was envisaged in the image of the fruit:

> O fruto de granada, recio afuera,
> Mas propicio y jugoso en lo escondido.
> Así, Escorial, te mira mi recuerdo.
> Si hacia los cielos anchos te alzas duro,
> Sobre el agua serena del estanque
> Hecho gracia sonríes. Y las nubes
> Coronan tus designios inmortales.

With the Escorial as the focal point for the meditation, the poet then broadened his reminiscence to a commentary on his own life outside of Spain:

> Porque me he perdido
> En el tiempo lo mismo que en la vida,
> Sin cosa propia, fe ni gloria,
> Entre gentes ajenas
> Y sobre ajeno suelo
> Cuyo polvo no es el de mi cuerpo;
> ... ...
> A ti, Escorial, me vuelvo.

This manipulation of a physical object in order to derive further consequences and applications to the spiritual state of the poet is a hallmark of what we have termed the meditative poetry of Cernuda. The poet has not yet achieved a mastery in using poetic voices: this rather discursive poem continually makes use of remembrance and self-address that is one-dimensional; that is to say that it is still very much poetry of the first voice, using Eliot's terminology. While it would be unjust to call the poetry of the first voice merely "confessional" poetry, there is, in this instance, a lack of objectification of experience; the poem wavers between the symbolic import of the Escorial and the poet's spiritual state. In a word, the symbol does not carry the burden of the poet's argument without the poet speaking in the first person, confirming the symbol's relevance.

T. S. Eliot's "third voice," on the other hand, supplies the necessary objectivity that enables the poet to divorce his own self from his creation. With this new-found freedom, he can delineate a character which is totally alien to his own self, and thus carry out a trenchant criticism by having this same character embody all that the poet wishes to censure. In Cernuda's second attempt to encompass the theme of the Escorial, we shall note a traversal from the first to the third poetic voice, for the poem that we are about to analyze begins resolutely in the person of Philip the Second, who speaks as he views the construction of the Escorial from his throne, "la silla del rey," which still affords to the viewer the unique perspective from which the Escorial should be seen: from above.

In contrast to the only partially realized symbolism of the Escorial in "Ruiseñor sobre la piedra," the poem, "Silla del rey" has a more urgent and concentrated formulation of the spirit of the edifice. If we were to characterize the theme of this poem, it would be that of unity: unity of the fate of the world with that of the universe, of the forces of the state under a single king, who forged out of the most heterogeneous peoples and ambitions a unique vision of a political and religious force. The Escorial embodies this to the greatest degree. Given the fact that the poet envisions it as evidence of the glory and the folly of Spain, it is not surprising that he should return again to the theme, but this time in the *persona* of Philip the Second, the architect of forcefully imposed unity of intent with realization, applying as much to the empire as to the Escorial. The unitive impulse that Cernuda sees in Philip's monument in stone is the fate of Spain.

In the earlier poem, the edifice was represented by two images: the fruit, previously cited, which suggests a hidden core of strength within a forbidding exterior. The succeeding image of

> Si hacia los cielos anchos te alzas duro,
> Sobre el agua serena del estanque
> Hecho gracia sonríes...

suggests a horizontal unification of opposites, in that the view from on high gives a greater impression of warmth and humanity than the perspective gained by observing it on the ground. The perspective not only satisfies God, but the grace and massive power of the Escorial are no less apparent to man. The same play of opposites will characterize Philip's opening words in "Silla del rey":

> Aquí sentado miro cómo crece
> La obra, dulce y dura, vasta y una,
> Protegiendo, tras el muro de piedra,
> La fe, mi diamante de un más claro día,
> Tierra hecha luz, la luz en nuestros hechos

The same set of opposing qualities appears in both poems. The interior of the monastery is characterized as "Le fe, mi diamante de un más claro día," which corresponds to the inner core of the fruit, "...recio afuera, / Mas propicio y jugoso en lo escondido." The walls protect the practice and the tenets of Catholicism, standing as militant defenders of a transcendent faith. The opposites found in both poems are not in conflict or contradiction with each other, but are rather extremes which the edifice encompasses. They are the outer and inner limits, the polarities which complement each other: "dulce y dura, vasta y una."

Once the total governing power of the architect-king is impressed upon us, the monologue continues to document the semidivine powers of the king. Beginning with the omnipotence of the ruler over his kingdom, the poem proceeds to detail greater regal dominions — Spain and its subjection to the king's power:

> La luz no es mía, sino la tierra sólo,
> La tierra díscola y diversa, que yo ahora
> Tengo bajo mi brazo y siento doblegarse,
> Fuerza febril, felina y femenina,
> Nula por mi poder, pero latente.

Philip's command over the design and the form of the edifice is only a prefiguration of the absolute mastery over Spain that is his. The country's diverse impulses are directed and disciplined toward a divine end, just as the elements that embody the structure of the monastery are utilized for an ultra-terrestrial design. The spiritual attitude that the Escorial belies is not due to any innate sense of the Divine on the part of Philip's subjects. Rather, his design, channels the brute and latent forces within Spain to a higher plane:

> Acaso nadie excepto yo noticie
> Por el aire tranquilo de mis pueblos,
> El furor de la fiera a quien cadenas forjo,
> Codicioso del mal, y cuya presa
> Extremada sería el sueño que edifico.

The unity which the all-powerful king fashions out of the free diversity and disparity among his peoples finally reaches its culmination in the tripartite formula: one monarch, one empire, one sword. [5] "El imperio está aquí, como juguete / Rutilante a mis pies; la espada, iris y rayo, / Por mi mano la llevan capitanes." The single entity that stems from these three forces is the all-encompassing prerogative of the king. The Escorial is the keystone to Philip's conscious effort to raise himself above other men, to make myth out of the stuff of his country and his religion:

> Todo traza mi trama, va hacia el centro
> Austero y áulico, corazón del Estado,
> Adonde llega, como la sangre de las venas,
> Para inspirarse e informarse, convertido
> En fluir no mortal de leyenda y de historia.

Within the constrictions that the king imposes on his country and his people, they are totally free, like a convict who has the run

---

5   Hernando de Acuña, "Al rey nuestro señor."

of a prison. The subtle and potent discipline imposed by the king gives the people the necessary framework for belief and accomplishment. Without this, Philip maintains, there can be nothing but anarchy and chaos in the kindgdom:

> En acto y en idea la vida ya se ajusta
> A mi canon católica, por campos,
> Por ciudades, por mares transitables
> Hasta tierras de allende, oscuras descubiertas,
> Y el hombre es libre en mí, como yo en él soy siervo.

The vast spectrum of humanity that Spain offers to the king, that "tierra díscola y diversa" which he spoke of earlier must inevitably undergo a reduction of its being. Idiosyncracies and extremes of human behavior must be stamped out so that the total plan of the king may be carried out without protest from a recalcitrant individual. The will of the king must be made a reality; the mythification is yet another weapon in forging the heterogeneous ambitions of the people into a common cause.

> Maté a la variedad, y ésa es mi gloria,
> Si alguna gloria puede reivindicar el hombre
> Por singular que su estación le haga,
> Como la mía. Ninguno igual a mí por el orgullo
> Y la humildad, que me hacen monarca con dos faces

This combination of prostration before the will of God and an attendant pride in being the one chosen to carry it out impels the king to *be* well beyond what he in fact *is*. His indomitable will forces him to assume a divine and inhuman perspective over his monastery and his empire. All events and actions must now be seen *sub specie aeternitatis*. The king must be the agent of divine will on earth, he cannot allow himself the weaknesses of other men. The monastery of the Escorial is exactly the constructive figuration of this union of ascetic humility and superhuman pride:

> La expresión de mi ser contradictorio,
> Que se exalta por sentirse inhumano,
> Que se humilla por sentirse imposible,
> Este muro la cifra, entre el verdor adusto,
> La sierra gris, los claros aires.

Out of the contradictions of the self, out of the raw mass of potential which was the Spain of his day, a total concordance results from each individual's ambition: all elements are directed and sanctioned by the all-seeing and clairvoyant king. This accord among divergent souls makes for a "harmony" within the imagination of the king, resulting from the union of different men and ideals under the force of a transcendent religious ideal, in comparison to which all their lives are nothing:

> Una armonía total, irresistible, surge;
> Colmena de musical dulzor, resuena todo;
> Es en su celda el fraile, donde doma el deseo;
> En su campo el soldado, donde forja la fuerza;
> En su espejo el poeta, donde refleja el mito.

This ideal, although a transcendental one, may well be a chimera. It is difficult to imagine Philip himself doubting his own mission, but Cernuda's "Philip" is another matter; it is clear that the poet wishes to suggest that the whole Catholic ideal that Philip embodies may yet be another example of man's propensity for absurd and quixotic idealism:

> Sé que estas vidas, por quienes yo respondo,
> En poco servirían de no seguir unidas
> Frente a una gran tarea, grande aunque absurda;
> Su voluntad a solas no asintiendo
> Con voluntad contigua. Mi cetro es su cayado.

The tendency to make no differentiation among ideals, to be ready to sacrifice oneself for any cause beyond the mere task of living, constitutes the burden of the next strophe. The lack of critical acumen is compensated by a stoic ability to abide by all the misfortune that their folly brings upon them:

> Envidiosos, ilógicos, rebeldes,
> Aptos a querellarse con sus sombras,
> Por palabra ingeniosa de su mal distraídos,
> Que aprecian igualmente el andrajo y el ámbar,
> Y en triunfo y ruina hallan igual reposo.

Philip's visionary mind provides for his people the impulse and the opportunity to gather from the natural world the riches that await them. Their duty is limited to this, and not to a doubting of the viability of the enterprise or its ultimate worth. In Philip's own words, he is a humble gardener who must not question his station in life, but silently reap whatever the people offer him:

> Pero el buen hortelano a la tierra que tiene
> No la discute, sino saca el fruto;
> Y yo de tierra mala trazo un huerto
> Sellado para el mundo todo,
> Que huraño lo contempla concertando hundirlo.

Philip, seated on the *silla del rey*, cannot fulfill or realize any greater ambition than the structure that is taking form in the valley below him. From the perspective of the mountain above the edifice, Philip contents himself with his own station, just as the ignorant peasant should be content with his. To request a higher station on earth would encroach upon God's duties — only He can parcel out man's fate while on earth. The king is thus wholly satisfied with his mission, his godlike mastery over men and time:

> Mas tras de mí, ¿qué reserva la suerte
> Para mi obra? Subir más no es posible,
> Sino quedar en el cenit, adonde
> Como astro que se vea
> Para glosa y por gloria de los siglos futuros.

The impregnable stone gives assurance to Philip that he has accomplished as much against the ravages of time as is given to any man. In this strictly temporal sense, the Escorial is a monument to the immutable and changeless thirst for belief which moves Philip as much as any other man. Only he could realize the vaguely-sensed ambition and bring it into reality through this edifice. Willfully, he insists that it will live, for it is not only stone, but the spirit made mute and changeless by its embodiment in stone. The spirit does not perish, neither can the stone, which is the exterior representation of the former:

> La mutación es mi desasosiego,
> Que victorias de un día en derrotas se cambien.
> Mi reino triunfante ¿ha de ver su ruina?
> O peor pesadilla ¿vivirá sólo en eco,
> Como en concha vacía vive el mar consumido?

> Mi obra no está afuera, sino adentro,
> En el alma; y el alma, en los azares
> Del bien y el mal, es igual a sí misma:
> Ni nace, ni perece. Y esto que yo edifico
> No es piedra, sino alma, el fuego inextinguible.

Philip's "fire" made stone symbolizes the unrelenting physical power of dogma over spirit. Once the spirit is embodied in stone, it becomes rigid, hardly bespeaking the gentle voice and the disdain of institutions that Christ displays in the Gospels. The world is thus divided between those who defend the dogma that the Escorial embodies and those who defend a freer kind of belief: these are the heretics. They must be expunged, for they shatter the unity of purpose which, although factitious, still serves to order the world:

> El fuego encierra al dogma y el dogma encierra al hombre.
> Aquellos que otra cosa defendieran
> Son ilusos heréticos, aunque clamen amparo
> En Cristo. César es quien conviene
> Lo que es suyo y de Cristo.

The perfect parable of Christ returning to earth again only to be martyred by the institution that He created and founded is that of the Grand Inquisitor from Dostoyevsky's The Brothers Karamazov. Cernuda employs it here, but the Inquisitor is Philip himself. [6]

> Cuando Alguno en Su nombre regresara al mundo
> Que por Él yo administro, encontraría,
> Conclusa y redimida, la obra ya perfecta;
> Intento de cambiarla ha de ser impostura,
> Y a Su impostor, si no la cruz, la hoguera aguarda.

---

[6] Dostoyevsky's inquisitor makes the same complaint as that of Philip — the coming of Christ only disturbs the faithful and disrupts the unity of belief, and so He must be crucified again. "I repeat, tomorrow Thou shalt see that obedient flock who at a sign from me will hasten to heap up the hot cinders about the pile on which I shall burn Thee for coming to hinder us. For if any one has ever deserved our fires, it is Thou. Tomorrow I shall burn Thee. Dixi." The Brothers Karamazov, Trans., Constance Garnett. (New York, 1950), p. 309.

Philip's earlier portrayal of himself and his mission on earth as "...una gran tarea, grande aunque absurda" returns in the form of the infallibility of the king. He maintains that his errors automatically become truths, for he represents Christ who, by his own definition, cannot err.

> No puedo equivocarme, no debo equivocarme;
> Y aunque me equivocase haría
> El que mi error se tornara
> Verdad, pues que mi error no existe
> Sino por Él, y por Él acertando me equivoco.

This sophistry of power is the unique basis for Philip's command over the world. The Escorial becomes not only the concretion of belief and a bastion against time, but a testimonial to the folly of men and their urge to believe:

> Manos atareadas van alzando la obra,
> Que viva aquí, en la mente, ha de vivir lo mismo
> Para el mundo exterior, sin mudar el oriente
> Del sueño pensativo, sin perder la pureza
> Que como voluntad siento inflexible.

> Y el futuro será, inmóvil, lo pasado:
> Imagen de esos muros en el agua.

> (*RD.*, pp. 264-267.)

In contrast to the fluctuation between the poet's thought and the symbolism of the Escorial noted in the earlier poem, this monologue explicitly carries out its purpose as expressed by Cernuda: "...proyectar mi experiencia emotiva sobre una situación dramática, histórica o legendaria... para que así se objetivara mejor, tanto dramática como poéticamente." [7] This objectivity is achieved by the choice of a historical character rather alien to the sympathies of the poet. The poet intentionally wants to take a critical stance toward the problem of Spain. Instead of a purely polemical poem (such as he was later to write in *Desolación de la quimera*), the poet reversed what might be poetic negativism into a positive dramatic figure — his Philip embodies Spain. The king is a poetic

---

[7] Cernuda, *Poesía y literatura*, pp. 261-262.

incarnation of Cernuda's innermost negative convictions. Philip's train of thought is alien to Cernuda, but this quality reveals all that the poet wishes to censure.

In the poem "Quetzalcóatl," the transformation of a simple man, *un espectador,* into a lawless accomplice of the rage to conquer was the burden of Cernuda's argument. The dominance which Cortés exerted over the Aztecs was that of a prideful man who imposed his will upon a submissive populace. In "Silla del rey," the power is wielded in the name of Christ, but the figure of God on earth is actually anathema to Philip, who realizes that the easy informality and generosity of Christ's spirit could hardly be tolerated within the confines of church and state, as controlled by the king. His wish that unity be achieved through the exercise of temporal power is, in effect, a Procrustean plan that will give form to the amorphous mass of humanity. The prerogative of the king brings about his own inhumanity, for he himself knows that he has to be more mythic than any other man if he is to rule. This absorption with the divine mission precludes a concern for the individual, and it is here that the king and the pillager become one. Although it would be inaccurate to equate the figures of Cortés, Bernal Díaz, and Philip, Cernuda certainly derives similar conclusions from all three, for they all inflict cruelty and suffering upon men through a strict and obstinate application of the force of their own indomitable wills. It is no matter that the ends envisaged are dissimilar. One works for riches and glory, the other labors for the reign of the spirit on earth: both are ruthless in their manipulation of the individual to the respective end.

Until now, we have read two monologues, one of which treats of power for the aggrandizement of the self ("Quetzalcóatl"), the other for the other-worldly ends which the protagonist envisioned for his country ("Silla del rey"). In the following poem, this trilogy of power is completed by the poem entitled "El César": power is employed not only for personal gain but for the furtherance of the fortunes of the state. Caesar embodies the kind of power that is wielded for a political abstraction.

In contrast to the figures of Cortés, Bernal Díaz, and Philip the Second, the Caesar that Cernuda creates through the device of the monologue is not moved by ascetic ideals or a distrust of what is immediately pleasurable. Quite the contrary, he delights in sensual pleasure and the irrational use of the power at his disposal much in the style of some of the demonic eccentrics that abound in Suetonius' *Lives of the Caesars*. The solitude that power imposes upon those who wield it forms the opening theme of the poem. The dictator finds himself a captive within his own empire, trusting no one and daring not to extend his friendship for fear of betrayal:

> Isla, en su roca escarpada inaccesible,
> Segura; sola morada para el César, como
> El César sólo ser para morar en ella.
> ... ...
> Todo aquí en soledad, a solas
> Como conciencia en alta noche,
> Mas libre de su angustia. Seguro
> Estoy de que la faz humana, ya insoportable
> Tiranía, no romperá esta magia.
> La ciudad está lejos, y un sueño en su memoria,...

In spite of the ostensible calm, the dictator is aware of the plotting and the hopes for revenge that surround him. Unlike Cortés or Philip, Caesar's life is completely taken up with the acquisition of power, his energies are directed only to the preservation of the status quo. The thralldom of the people has no object other than the conservation of the dictator's ego. Alone on his island, the despot is able to contemplate from afar the hordes beneath his command and thereby derive a spurious sense of his own superiority. He has no religious ideal that might transcend the exercise of power, nor does he possess the avaricious egotism and masculine thirst for exploration and discovery that animated Cortés. Caesar's life is the nihilistic utilization of power for no other objective than self-gratification:

> Conmigo estoy, yo el César, dueño
> Mío, y en mí del mundo. Mi domino
> De lo visible abarca a lo invisible,
> Cerniendo como un dios, pues que divino soy
> Para el temor y el odio de humanas criaturas,
> Las dos alas gemelas del miedo y la esperanza.
> Pero ¿es cierta esta calma? ¿No hay zozobra
> Entre las ramas de un puñal al acecho?

His mental inertia does not bring about a distraction from the thought of his final end by assassination. The calm serenity which he senses around him may well foreshadow his death. Worse, still, he is no longer able to sleep, for the dreams that bring the past before his mind prevent a serene and contemplative rest:

> Lejos aún está la madrugada
> Con su insomnio tenaz, o su visita
> De horribles sueños, que me cuestan
> Lágrimas y gemidos. Mas no debo
> Pensar en eso, sino mirar las rosas
> Cándidas y lascivas, ...

There is a curious relationship between the pleasure that the Caesar seeks and the power that he wields, for his pleasure is decidedly increased in the knowledge that he may order the death of the being that gives him pleasure, reminding us of a similar fantasy of the Marquis de Sade.

> Al besar una boca, el pensamiento
> De que aquella cabeza caería
> Si una palabra digo, aún extiende
> Mi gozo más allá de sus fronteras
> Naturales. ¿Acaso al cuerpo de que se goza
> Una tortura no imponemos?

The self-absorption with his station and the exploitation of the power that he wields is not enough, however, to prevent the encroachments of time from having an effect upon him. The illusions that he has of his still-remaining youth are nothing but sheer fantasy, but the true import of his advancing age gradually impresses itself upon him. "...El tiempo con su apremio extreme / La carga que doblega y que pretendo / Arrojar. Ilusiones aún: la vida es otra cosa." Nature, surrounding the despot on his island, always is an irrevocable sign of passing time, and he cannot deny it:

> A oscuras, oigo en mi yacija
> La lluvia, el surtidor, el oleaje,
> Batiendo contra el mármol o la roca,
> Resucitar parecen las aguas del pasado,
> Que vuelven y me ahogan, lentas, irreprimibles.

Caesar's conclusions about the subject of power are not surprising: it is for young men who are still able to throw themselves into the deceptive permanence that it seems to offer. For an aging tyrant, it is only an impediment to a quiet old age and a peaceful death. The gradual corruption of the spirit begins with the dictator, still young, revelling in honors and acclaim from the mob:

> Propósitos perdidos del mozo generoso
> A quien temple y destino hostigan de consuno.
> Cuando laurel y púrpura eran gratos
> Tras hazaña de armas o togas,
> Que las picas de hierro y el bronce de los haces
> Orillan. Cuando marfil y cedro iban
> Entre la multitud mecidos,
> Como nave entre olas, al estruendo
> De las gargantas agrias, donde suena
> La música brutal del populacho,
> Cuyo admirar y odiar ciego confunde.

No one but Caesar has ever enjoyed such power, but its use is not only sensually pleasurable, "la tácita oferta de todo el ser, en alma / Y cuerpo, lo terreno y lo celeste," but sadistically so, which is in its own way a kind of pleasure given only to a Caesar, and that in the grandest and most orgiastic scale imaginable.

What is there in common among Cortés, Philip the Second and Caesar? Above all, there is the distance between themselves and their subjects, that curious abstraction from reality that the exercise of power imposes on those who possess it. This distance affords them a divine and inhuman perspective over the world, a callousness toward mankind which is little consolation for their total alienation from the reality around them. The conqueror and the ruler are semi-mythic personages who partake of many of the attributes of the Divinity. For instance, in Cernuda's re-creation of Philip the Second, the poet molded the king in order to represent in microcosm the macrocosm that is the Almighty. This "divine distance" between reality and the ruler is just the substance of Caesar's thoughts at this point:

> El poder, ¿quién ha de conocerlo
> Como yo? El poder que corrompe
> Espíritu, como una enfermedad oculta

> Corrompe carne. Pero aun así, divino
> Es, que aislado me destina
> A ver las criaturas allá lejos,
> Lo mismo que las ve el águila en el aire.
> Grandeza corrompida que arrastra y que levanta,
> Mantiene en equilibrio este mortal residuo
> De mi existir, tan desmedido y flaco.

Still, this semi-divine existence, like all stations in life, has its lights and shadows, and the ruler must be continually aware of the hordes that are intent upon his downfall, the rustling of the curtains or the foliage which might augur an assassination:

> Mas suena sigilosa una pisada,
> La seda reticente en la cortina;
> Me obsesiona un rumor inexistente
> A toda hora. El poder no corrompe,
> Enloquece y aísla.

The negative side of the ruler's solitude is the alienation from other men that he freely brings upon himself through the acceptance of the throne. The spectacle that lies before his mind's eye of murder and intrigue finally makes him conclude that he can trust no one, that all men are his enemies. We see again that power has an analogous effect upon all those who exercise it, regardless of the codes of morality or immorality to which the rulers ascribe. The king, above men, is inevitably a stranger to the people he rules:

> Es la sangre, tanta sangre vertida;
> Su rumor ¿no sube por los aires,
> Clamando en vano? Tanta muerte,
> De amigos y de extraños, administrada con veneno
> O con puñal; súbita asombrando
> O demorada, por mejor conocerla.
> ¿Amigos, dije? Amante o familiar, extraños todos.

The nihilistic revelling in bloodshed is the final obsession of Caesar, for only he can formulate a code of immorality. He is above the law; his lawlessness makes him the unique beneficiary: the rest of humanity must be the victim:

Inocentes, lavadas en su blancura vieja,
Como las de una virgen que hilara y que rezara
Ajena al mundo, al animal espasmo
Emparejado. En vano las pregunto; no conocen
Ellas ni nadie el beneficio de la sangre vertida.
La víctima provoca al verdugo inocente,
Y la sangre no acusa, la sangre es beneficio
Mayor, necesaria igual que el agua es a la tierra.

(*RD.*, pp. 274-278.)

Our main purpose in analyzing the three poems that form the
basis of this chapter is to delineate Cernuda's gradual progress
toward the ideal of non-subjective poetry that will more and
more tend to make use of dramatic or historical characters to
enforce the objective quality of the thoughts of the speaker.
This technique is quite common among English poets who are
roughly contemporary to Cernuda. T. S. Eliot, for instance, whom
Cernuda has studied assiduously, affirmed as early as 1919 that
"poetry is not a turning loose of emotion, but an escape from
emotion; it is not the expression of personality, but an escape
from personality." [8] The projection of the emotive experience of
the poet, therefore, is a kind of escape from the self, an effort to
make the poetry relevant and meaningful through a mythification
of poetic material. The *personae* shoud not be considered as
different facets of the poet, but rather as dramatic creations of
his imagination which are only tenuously related to the poet's
own body of belief. The *persona* represents the focal point for
the poet's criticism of reality: the created character's positive
statements derive from the poet's convictions. While delineating
the despot or the rapacious conqueror, the poet reveals his own
inner revulsion toward them. The relevance of the mask to the
poet is a disputed point. Yeats related the creation of the mask
to the matter of poetic discipline: "If we cannot imagine ourselves
as different from what we are and assume that second self, we
cannot impose a discipline upon ourselves, though we may accept
one from others. Active virtue as distinguished from the passive

---

[8] T. S. Eliot, "Tradition and the Individual Talent," in *Selected Essays*
(New York, 1950), p. 10.

acceptance of a current mode is therefore theatrical, consciously dramatic, the wearing of a mask." [9]

Cernuda affiirms this and adds more in his essay on Yeats: "Pero la palabra (máscara) tiene otro sentido... el de ser la máscara un arma para defendernos y que no nos hagan daño, algo interpuesto entre la vida y nosotros. Puede ser, también, un arma de ataque, signo de un ideal heroico de nosotros mismos." [10] Like all generalizations, the opposite view has its supporters, too: "Desde un punto de vista psicológico, la máscara manifiesta que un hombre quiere mostrar, sin ser él identificado, un modo de ser —lujuria, sadismo, altanería, sarcasmo, etc.— más o menos reprimido en su alma cuando los demás reconocen su real identidad." [11]

On yet another plane, the mask, "...uno de los inventos más antiguos de la humanidad, manifiesta la constitutiva aspiración del hombre a ser todo lo que su limitación le impide ser." [12]

The character of Lazarus in the poem contained a considerable fund of experience from the poet's own life — his show this. But that was the only occasion where the poet indicated any relation between himself and the historical or legendary characters in those long poems. In this regard, one can only recur to the implications drawn by Laín Entralgo in his commentary on the relevance of the mask to the person who creates and wields it.

Still, there is no reason to avoid pointing out the strange coincidence between Cernuda's avowed distaste for the expression of the emotions —his "pudor"— and the corresponding interest in dramatic techniques through which the poet might speak at a distance. In general, the masks of Cernuda are at the same time critiques of the self, keen scrutinies of power and dominance over other men. It does not seem entirely accidental that the *personae* of Cernuda are, by reason of their own commanding positions as rulers or conquerors, above the normal run of humanity. Philip's aerial perspective while seated on the *silla del rey* is a physical confirmation in space of his own spiritual and political ascendancy

---

[9]   Yeats, *Autobiography,* pp. 400-401.
[10]   Cernuda, *Poesía y literatura II,* p. 178.
[11]   Pedro Laín Entralgo, *Teoría y realidad del otro* (Madrid, 1961), II, p. 137.
[12]   *Ibid.*

over men. He is semi-divine; he works the will of God on earth, instructing and directing the ignorant mass of humanity. To be above men, to be an agent of the divine among men, is very much a part of Cernuda's own aspiration. In Ortega's words, "...la conciencia de su propia relatividad... es en el hombre inseparable de la conciencia postuladora de lo absoluto. Y entonces se engendra en él el vehemente y equívoco afán de ser lo que no es: lo absoluto; participar de esa otra realidad superior..." [13]

In the poem "Lázaro," this "afán" which Ortega speaks of is not really relevant to the poem, for Lázaro is not the person that Cernuda wishes to be or to censure; quite the contrary, the Biblical figure is another representation of the self, more relevant to a reader than a poem written in the first person. The masks of Cernuda are not simple disguises, though; they embody aspects of reality that fascinate him.

The poetry of the mask is therefore imaginative and dramatic. The characters that the poet creates, like those in the theatre, are other beings with autonomous existence who expand the poet's imaginative capabilities by forcing him to imagine the actions and the passions of a character alien to the poet. They also have an analogous effect upon the reader, for they bring us into contact with a person who speaks to us from the poetry alone, a voice that is completely centered upon the self. This broadening ability of the *personae* has been accurately described by Walter Kaufmann: "poets are not philosophical oracles. Yet they have not only the gift of lending expression to single feelings and attitudes but also the power to create characters, enabling the reader to gain experiences for which any possibility would otherwise be lacking in a single human life. Poetry makes possible a vast expansion of our world, an extension of sympathy, and a profounder understanding not only of human possibilities but also of human realities." [14] Thus the creation of dramatic characters is the final step in a long process of self-realization and consciousness. If the poetry of Cernuda began with a narcissism which he was later to condemn, it developed even later into an abandonment

13 As cited in *Ibid.*
14 Walter Kaufmann, *From Shakespeare to Existentialism* (Garden City, 1960), p. 278.

of the self and the consequent creation of others, the *personae*.

The importance of these roles in the development of Cernuda's late poetry should be clear. They are a means of liberating the self from the emotions through an imaginative character, and then speaking as if the character himself were speaking. The poet evokes this fiction, whom he has never known or met, existing uniquely through the medium of literature. It is the "vehicle" for the poet's own sense of alienation from man and Nature. The historical or legendary aspects of the character are re-created from within the sensibility of the poet, with only a minimal interest shown in realizing a portrait which would conform to some kind of historical accuracy. So that there is a peculiar sense of interchange and identification in the use of this technique; in any case, there is no reason to attempt to make a final attribution for the thoughts of the character. What is evident is the new liberty and assurance of Cernuda's poetic voice — the poet can now approach and even express states of minds and attitudes that would be beyond the realm of his own voice. [15]

Cernuda chose such figures because of his impulse to censure, from his own personal point of view, the three "realities" which he knew through his own life experience: Spain in America, the power of dogma over Spain, and the whole subject of Spain itself, and finally the proliferation of dictators which he himself witnessed in the pre-war years. He achieves true *satire* by the use of the monologue, but we should understand the term not in the jocular sense, but rather as fully developed and serious consideration, and ultimate rejection of, the particular world view of each *persona*.

---

[15]   Jiménez, *Cinco Poetas del Tiempo*, p. 120.

VII

THE FINAL PHASE: THE OTHER

The dramatic characters created by Cernuda have only a tenuous relation to the self of the poet, but at the same time they cannot be clinically analyzed and isolated from the man Cernuda; there is a continual dialogue between the character and its maker. A similar kind of projection of the self took place in the poems about Nature, where the poet consciously wished to deny himself the life that was his and instead become one with the "all" that is creation. This life was still a kind of immortality for the poet but a futile and vicarious one, since the projections take place completely within the mind wishfully going out into Nature. The poet knows that it remains while the man who observes these things is doomed. The projections take various forms, and contain a fluctuating degree of identity with the poet. The dramatic figures in the last Chapter are not Cernuda, but they are tangentially related to him. Finally, there is another kind of projection: the creation by the poet of the "other," a figment of the poetic imagination which is, on the most elementary plane, the poet's double. There exists an intimate relation between the projected voice, the *persona*, and the pure existence of the "other." This process, which might be termed an atomization of the ego into separate and autonomous other selves, is actually an acerbated consciousness of the self. "Self consciousness, as the term is ordinarily used, implies two things: an awareness of oneself by oneself, and an awareness of oneself as an object of someone else's observation." [1] It is probable that Baudelaire's *homo duplex* is the closest approximation that we have to a definition of the ruinous effects of self-consciousness upon the person. A condition of solitude is basic for the meditation upon the self and the consequent creation of other selves. The introspection is a fruitful one, for man alone suddenly finds himself with "others" in this imagination. "Quien se ha sentido radicalmente solo es que tiene la capacidad de estar radicalmente acompañado. Al sentirme *solo*, me aparece la totalidad de cuanto hay, en tanto que me falta. En la verdadera soledad están *los otros* más presentes que nunca." [2] The self alone is the key to the imaginative making of the "other." Kierkegaard, fervently read by Cernuda, is capital in this regard: "Kierkegaard ... noted that the 'single one' is a category through which the self must pass during the course of a dialectic by which the self finds the self." [3] The state of the 'single one' has been something of a constant throughout the life and poetry of Cernuda. But the words "solitude" or "loneliness" hardly encompass the transcendental insolation of the self that characterizes Cernuda and his poetry. [4] Rather, let us use Philip Silver's phrase — "ontological solitude." This state has been brilliantly described by R. D. Laing:

> The individual in the ordinary circumstances of living may feel more unreal than real; in a literal sense, more dead than alive; precariously differentiated from the rest of the world, so that his identity and autonomy are always in question. He may lack the experience of his own temporal continuity. He may not possess an over-riding sense of personal consistency or cohesiveness. He may feel

---

1   R. D. Laing, *The Divided Self* (Chicago, 1960), p. 113.

2   Xavier Zubiri, as cited in Laín Entralgo, *Teoría y realidad*, p. 133.

3   Wylie Sypher, *Loss of the Self in Modern Literature and Art* (New York, 1962), p. 17.

4   "La soledad está en todo para ti, y todo para ti está en la soledad. Isla feliz adonde tantas veces te acogiste, compenetrado mejor con la vida y con sus designios... entre los otros y tú, entre el amor y tú, entre la vida y tú, está la soledad. Mas esa soledad, que de todo te separa, no te apena. ¿Por qué habría de apenarte? Cuenta hecha con todo, con la tierra, con la tradición, con los hombres, a ninguno debes tanto como a la soledad. Poco o mucho, lo que tú seas, a ella se lo debes." Luis Cernuda, *Ocnos* (Madrid, 1949), pp. 98-99.

more insubstantial than substantial, and unable to assume that the stuff he is made of is genuine, good, valuable. And he may feel his self as partially divorced from his body. [5]

A sense of identity is not automatically supplied by one's own body. "...It appears that bodily identity cannot be the criterion of personal identity and is at best only contingently correlated with it... real criteria of personal identity... must be "mental" or "psychological" criteria that a person can know to be satisfied in his own case quite apart from knowing anything about his body." [6] What is described here contains much of the existential state of *Geworfenheit* which was strikingly prefigured in Cernuda's own words: "I fell into the world." Within this state of ontological solitude, it is only the experience of communication, of which love is the highest manifestation, that enables the poet to continue living. In a state of physical solitude, the ontological state is aggravated to the point of desperation. The "other" is an invention of the poet: *it* observes him and speaks to him, serves as an object for his meditation. In one of Cernuda's preferred poems from among the classics of Spanish literature, the "Epístola a Arias Montano" of Francisco de Aldana, we find the same recourse to solitude and subsequent dialogue with the self:

---

[5] Laing, *The Divided Self*, p. 43.

[6] Sydney Shoemaker, *Self Knowledge and Self Identity* (Ithaca, 1963), pp. 123-34. One of the most humane expositions of the Yo-tú dialectic is contained in the chapters entitled "Los otros y yo" and "El peligro del otro y la sorpresa que es yo" from Ortega's late work entitled *El hombre y la gente*. "... hay en cada uno de nosotros un altruísmo básico que nos hace estar *a nativitate* abiertos al otro, al *alter* como tal. Este otro es el hombre, por el pronte, el hombre o individuo indeterminado, el Otro cualquiera, del cual sé sólo que es mi "semejante," en el sentido de que es capaz de responderme con sus racciones en un nivel aproximadamente igual al de mis acciones, cosa que no me acontecía con el animal... La relación *Nosotros* es la primaria forma de relación social o socialidad. No importa cuál sea su contenido —el beso, el trancazo. *Nos* besamos y *nos* pegamos. Lo importante aquí es el *nos*. En él ya no vivo, sino que convivo. La realidad *nosotros* o nostridad puede llamarse con un vocablo más usadero: trato. En el trato que es el *nosotros*, si se hace frecuente, continuado, el Otro se me va perfilando." José Ortega y Gasset, *El hombre y la gente,* Volume II, (Madrid, 1964) p. 19.

Entrarme en el secreto de mi pecho
Y platicar en él mi interior hombre.
Do va, do está, si bive, o qué se ha hecho.

Y porque vano error mas no me assombre
En algun alto, y solitario nido
Pienso enterrar mi ser, mi vida y nombre

Y como sino huuiera aca nacido
Estar me alla qual Eco replicando
Al dulce son de Dios, del Alma oydo. [7]

This other self, then, is totally unembodied and imaginary, not to be confused with either the various projections that we have been analyzing, nor the desire for total absorption by the inanimate or the animate that we saw in the poems of "architectural" or "natural" thematics. The "other" is the final phase of an increasingly acute self-consciousness that manifests itself by a continual use of unnamed "other" figures. These complete the poet's image of himself; they supply the other perspective from which the poet may see himself "at a distance," as it were. "Cernuda está tan acostumbrado a vivir sólo de las creaciones de su propia mente —las cuales obedecen y se dejan regir mucho más fácilmente que los hombres—, que la compañía verdadera le molesta. La fraternidad y el amor no han sido más que intentos de evadirse de la soledad que aún no había de valorar como se merece." [8] Through the use of the imaginary other, he affirms his own identity. "Most identities require an other in and through a relationship with whom the self's identity is actualized." [9]

The problem demands a broader temporal perspective than that used in previous chapters. Certain poems of Cernuda's earlier period foreshadow the use of the "other" that will become ever more frequent in the later poetry. Wheter we define this "other" as a *desdoblamiento del yo poético* or a simple *doppelgänger* of the poet's own self, this usage forms an essential aspect of the late poetry of Cernuda. This chapter gives a chronological account

[7]   *Obras completas* (Madrid, 1953), p. 73.
[8]   Biruté Ciplijauskaite, *La soledad y la poesía española contemporánea* (Madrid, 1962), p. 213.
[9]   R. D. Laing, *The Self and Others* (Chicago, 1962), p. 70.

of the topic from the earliest instances to the final examples, especially the poem "Viendo volver." The creation of the "other" by the poet is a middle way between engulfment by the loved one and the total isolation and unrelatedness of ontological solitude — *Entfremdung*. The created figure is actually one enormous metaphor of the self, a unique means through which the poet might become another. This other is a quasi-being, owing its existence to the author.

The earliest examples of the "other" are clearly related to the imaginative creation of the loved one. Such is the case with the prose poem "Estaba tendido," where the poet simply imagines the presence of another beside him. Although it is hardly indicative of the myriad uses of the double that we shall witness in the later poetry, I include it here since it is one of the first efforts of the poet to create the antithesis to the self:

> Estaba tendido y tenía entre mis brazos un cuerpo como seda. Lo besé en los labios, porque el río pasaba por debajo. Entonces se burló de mi amor.
>
> Sus espaldas parecían dos alas plegadas. Lo besé en las espaldas, porque el agua sonaba debajo de nosotros. Entonces lloró al sentir la quemadura de mis labios.
>
> Era un cuerpo tan maravilloso que se desvaneció entre mis brazos. Besé su huella; mis lágrimas la borraron. Como el agua continuaba fluyendo, dejé caer en ella un puñal, un ala, y una sombra.
>
> De mi mismo cuerpo recorté otra sombra, que sólo me sigue a la mañana. Del puñal y el ala, nada sé.
>
> (*RD.*, p. 70.)

The poet specifies that the creature beside him is not only inexistent, but moreover is a kind of prefiguration of his other self, that double which is present so often in the poetry of Cernuda. "De mí mismo recorté otra sombra, que sólo me sigue a la mañana": the poet has imagined an "other" that is not himself, nor the embodiment of another person. This is the beginning of a gradual division of the self that brings with it the presence of this semi-existent and ambiguous figure. In a later phase, the "other" will divest itself of any amatory significance, and take autonomous form as an inherent part of the poetic world. Beginning with a simple replacement of the *amado ausente,* the poet gradually divorces the "other" from the union implied by love, and gives the imagined figure an independence and an autonomy that is devoid of sensual meaning.

One of the poet's primary concerns is the escape from the self through the beloved or the contemplation of Nature, giving him an existence that does not function with the vagaries of his body. In the later poem "Déjame esta voz," he makes the same demand for a denial of the sentient self, but this time it is not without an increasing realization of what he would lose by the suicidal drive to become one with the universe: actually, it is a euphemism for suicide.

> Me ahogué en fin, amigos;
> Ahora duermo donde nunca despierto.
> No saber más de mí mismo es algo triste;
> Dame la guitarra para guardar las lágrimas.
>
> (*RD.*, p. 74.)

In the same book containing the above poem, *Los placeres prohibidos,* there is an increasing use of the *tú* which is not directed to another, but rather to the poet himself; he views his own being from a distance, and comments upon the self that he observes. This is the *desdoblamiento del yo,* which will make the division of the self all the more apparent to the reader. As an example of this technique, "De qué país" begins with the poet clearly addressing himself, but the force of the poetic voice tends to make us consider the speaker of the poem as another interlocutor, an "other" who inquires of the poet,

> De qué país eres tú,
> Dormido entre realidades como bocas sedientas,
> Vida de sueños azuzados,
> Y ese duelo que exhibes por la avenida de los monumentos,
> Donde dioses y diosas olvidados
> Levantan brazos inexistentes o miradas marmóreas.

The poet questions the total meaning of his existence. He is not assured of a native country, nor of his own identity or function in the world, nor even a justification for remaning alive. What is

worse, these questions from the "other" tend to convince the poet
of his own exile from all things and beings. A kind of dialogue
within the self has taken place. The conclusions that are drawn
force the "other" to state categorically:

No podrás pues besar con inocencia,
Ni vivir aquellas realidades que te gritan con lengua inagotable.
Deja, deja, harapiento de estrellas;
Muérete bien a tiempo.

(RD., pp. 75-76.)

While tracing the vague beginnings of the use of the "other,"
we cited examples that established two distinct functions. The
first was that of a simple imaginative replacement of the beloved
by the poet alone in his solitude. This kind of "other" is not
strictly within the limits of the later usages, but it is undoubtedly
a tentative start of the process. These are the first instances that we
have of a "going beyond the self" (salir de sí mismo) that contrasts
vividly with the more narcissistic preoccupations of the earlier
poems, specifically the "Egloga, Elegía, Oda" of 1927-1928. The
second function is that of the *tú* usage, where the self addresses
the self through the medium of the imagined "other." In
personifications of this type, there are some technical variations.
In the prose poem "Sentado sobre un golfo de sombra," the
emptiness of the self is elaborated. "Sentado sobre un golfo de
sombra vas siendo ya sombra tú todo. Sombra tu cabeza, sombra
tu vientre, sombra tu vida misma... Cuida tu sombra; dentro de
tiempo ni sombra serás. Cuida tu pecho y tus sueños, cuida tu
cabeza, que ya es una nube que se pierde, como chal delicado,
en la tempestad orquestada." [10] The solitude of the poet, his lack
of worldly significance is exemplified by a purposeful diminution of
his body in the poem "Tu pequeña figura":

Tu pequeña figura, sola en algún camino,
Cae lentamente desde la luz,
Semejante a la arena desde un brazo,
Cuando la mano, poema perdido,
Abre diez estrellas sobre el otoño de rojiza resonancia.

(RD., pp. 76-77.)

---

[10] *RD,* p. 76.

The key poem for an understanding of the Cernudian uses of these "other" figures is "Veía sentado," a relatively complex poem in which the poet describes the alienation of the self and the subsequent division into two: the self which acts and functions within reality, the other, mute and inactive, but watchful and reproachful of the "original" self. In spite of its length, I shall copy it in its entirety, for the poem reveals in a concentrated form all the later developments which concern us in this chapter.

> Veía sentado junto al agua
> Con vago ademán de olvido,
> Veía las hojas, los días, los semblantes,
> El fondo siempre pálido del cielo,
> Conversando indiferentes entre ellos mismos.
>
> Veía la luz agitarse eficazmente,
> Un pequeño lagarto de visita,
> Las piedrecillas vanidosas
> Disputando el lugar a tristes hierbas.
>
> Veía reinos perdidos o quizá ganados,
> Veía mi juventud ni ganada ni perdida,
> Veía mi cuerpo distante, tan extraño
> Como yo mismo, allá en extraña hora.
>
> Veía los canosos muros disgustados
> Murmurando entre dientes sus vagas blasfemias,
> Veía más allá de los muros
> El mundo como can satisfecho,
> Veía al inclinarme sobre la verdad
> Un cuerpo que no era el cuerpo mío.
>
> Subiendo hasta mí mismo
> Aquí vive desde entonces,
> Mientras aguardo que tu propia presencia
> Haga inútil ese triste trabajo
> De ser yo solo el amor y su imagen.

(RD., pp. 82-83.)

The poem is marvelously deceptive for many reasons, primarily because of the two orthodox stanzas which open the poem. There is nothing at all strange in having the poet contemplate what he sees as he rests by a pool in an enclosed garden. If anything can be predicted in poetry, this kind of description of the objects in the world through the focus of the eye of the poet could hardly be more common. However, the third strophe introduces the Narcissus motif: the poet gazes at his own image in the pool. The myth carries with it not only the implications of a first awakening of physical desire that his own image arouses, but also of the first strains of a consciousness of the self, for what Narcissus sees in the pool is not only his first image of himself, but an "other" who is the object of his newly-found desire. Just as God needed Creation in order to define Himself, the poet must have a mirror to see himself through the "other." This poem by Cernuda is not a retelling of the myth; quite the contrary, it documents the poet's disenchantment with his own self and his consciousness which is totally at odds with the previous manifestations. The first indication that the "other" is present is indicated in the third strophe, where the poet finally becomes conscious of his reflection in the pool: "Veía mi cuerpo distante, tan extraño / Como yo mismo, allá en extraña hora." The poet senses himself alien to the image in the pool, yet one with it, for after all, it *is* himself! The possibilities for estrangement of the self do not end here: there is a temporal alienation implied in the phrase "allá en extraña hora" denoting all the more forcibly the divorce of the poet from the world around him, and the consequential alternative, which is a fascination with his own image. The fourth strophe prepares the reader for the final abandonment of the Narcissism with which the poet began. He leans over the pool, sees his total image: "Veía al inclinarme sobre la verdad / Un cuerpo que no era el cuerpo mío."

The fourth strophe describes the upward movement of the image in the pool into the body of the poet, so that it becomes one with it. The implications that the poet is no longer content with his own self-contemplation are quite evident. In fact, he abandons it by making the image unite with him. Yet, he still remains desirous of the "other," still wishes to see himself through the eyes of another. Consequently, he asks for a *third* presence, an object for his love which does not yet exist. If this figure were to appear, it would then render irrelevant and useless this vain task of being lover and beloved at the same time: "Mientras aguardo que tu propia presencia / Haga inútil este triste trabajo / De ser yo solo el amor y su imagen."

In this poem what have we witnessed but a victory over the self, a demand for a new relation with the "other"? If the inordinate introspection and fascination with the self has always been somewhat alien to the mature Cernuda, there is no doubt that this divorce from the self is not abrupt or unexpected; rather it was preceded by a gradual realization that the self alone is not enough, that the egotism implied by this totally self-centered poetic universe could end only in sterility and irrelevance. If one's consciousness only takes form through the eyes of the "other," and the poet remains alone, the self itself must create the "other." As we have already noted, this poem details in a remarkably vivid way the abandonment of the *yo* and the consequent search for the "other." The most elementary stage of this search is amatory. But as the ontological insecurity becomes more and more oppressive to the poet, this "other" will divest itself of any amatory significance and take on a greater and more significant autonomy.

All of the poems cited so far are taken from *Los placeres prohibidos,* published in 1931. The poem which immediately follows "Veía sentado" is entitled "He venido para ver," chosen by the poet to end the book, and with it a preliminary stage in the development of the "other." In this poem, the relation of the poet to the "other" is still figurative and illusory:

> Adiós, dulces amantes invisibles,
> Siento no haber dormido en vuestros brazos.
> Vine por esos besos solamente;
> Guardad los labios por si vuelvo.

> (*RD.,* p. 84.)

In the succeeding book of poems, *Donde habite el olvido* (1932-1933), the relation of the poet's self to the world and, by implication, to the "other" is still tenuous and intermittent. Nevertheless, the initial impulse to escape from the self and become one with the "other" is still discernible among the surrealistic dream states that the poet describes throughout the book. The most striking evidence of this desire to "perderse" in the "other" through the force of love is expressed in the second poem of this book, entitled "Como una vela sobre el mar":

Sintiendo todavía los pulsos de ese afán,
Yo, el más enamorado,
En las orillas del amor,
Sin que una luz me vea
Definitivamente muerto o vivo,
Contemplo sus olas y quisiera anegarme
Deseando perdidamente
Descender, como los ángeles aquellos por la escala de espuma,
Hasta el fondo del mismo amor que ningún hombre ha visto.

(RD., p. 88.)

Exactly the same "salir de sí mismo" is expressed in the following poem of the book. The poet now divorces himself from his substance, picturing his body as empty and without material existence. He interprets the reality around him as a chimera and an illusion, and attaches non-material attributes to it in order to express its spiritual desolation. At the same time, there is a vicarious imagining of the beloved; but since this hope is always thwarted, the "other" remains in the realm of the imagination, similar to the situations found in the last two poems of *Los placeres prohibidos*.

Esperé un dios en mis días
Para crear mi vida a su imagen,
Mas el amor, como un agua,
Arrastra afanes al paso.

Me he olvidado a mí mismo en sus ondas;
Vacío el cuerpo, doy contra las luces;
Vivo y no vivo, muerto y no muerto;
Ni tierra ni cielo, ni cuerpo ni espíritu.

(RD., p. 88.)

In a situation analogous to that of the poet, the figure of Adam, who has just been banished from Paradise, is described as seeking his own self in the same way. This search was not necessary while in Eden, for there was no need to *be*, no need to *live*, for the creatures of Heaven are without clocks and the attendant impulse to live intensely before death disrupts the short span of life:

Se buscaba a sí mismo,
Pretendía olvidarse a sí mismo;
Niño en brazos del aire,

> En lo más poderoso descansado,
> Mano en la mano, frente en la frente.
> Entre precipitadas formas vagas,
> Vasta estela de luto sin retorno,
> Arrastraba dos lentas soledades,
> Su soledad de nuevo, la del amor caído.
>
> (*RD.*, p. 93.)

The replacement of the beloved with the imagined "other" reaches a further development in the poem "Mi Arcángel," from the same book of poems. The archangel is the perfect symbol for the "other," since, according to Catholic belief, each soul on earth is given an archangel who accompanies the soul on its journey on earth, helps the sinner in his distress, and finally intercedes for him on the Day of Judgment. This archangel is an imaginative creation to whom the poet might speak, without having to recur again to the *amado de la imaginación* employed in the earlier poems. As was the case with the imagined lover, however, the archangel not only is an evidence of the poet's own solitude, but is a partner in the continual dialogue with the self. Cernuda addresses this celestial "other" with a considerable amount of deference and respect:

> Tú fluyes en mis venas, respiras en mis labios,
> Te siento en mi dolor;
> Bien vivo estás en mí, vives en mi amor mismo,
> Aunque a veces
> Pesa la luz, la soledad.

The archangel does not exist; a creation of the poet for the poet, it is a witness to the divinity of the artist among men:

> Vuelto en el lecho, como niño sin nadie frente al muro,
> Contra mi cuerpo creo,
> Radiante enigma, el tuyo;
> No ríes así ni hieres,
> No marchas ni te dejas, pero estás conmigo.

> Estás conmigo como están mis ojos en el mundo,
> Dueños de todo por cualquier instante;
> Mas igual que ellos, al hacer la sombra, luego vuelvo,
> Mendigo a quien despojan de su misma pobreza,
> Al yerto infierno de donde he surgido.
>
> (*RD.*, p. 96.)

The extension of the poet's desire for the beloved and the "other" through space is destroyed not only by the effects of time upon the physical person of the beloved, but also by the decay of emotion under the weight of boredom and passing time. The love which is imagined in the future is just the same as the love which exists as remembrance. The first is summarized by desire, which signifies the love has not yet been realized nor consummated. The second betokens nostalgia and *recuerdo,* but in either case the love is inexistent *at present;* the poet remains alone, seeking his own identity in an "other" who does not appear. Not finding it anywhere, he plunges further into an acute solipsistic state.

"Invocaciones" has within it the seeds for a novel renovation and renewal of the "other," containing even broader uses of the "other" than those seen heretofore in our brief survey of the technique in the earlier books. A poem from "Invocaciones" that is capital in this regard is the justly renowned "Soliloquio del farero," where Cernuda employs direct personification; in so doing, he creates the "other" which he must have in order that his poetry function as a dialogue within the mind. We recall the personified goddess of Melancholy in "Himno a la tristeza," but now we shall examine instead an earlier example from the same book of poems. The state of mind bespeaks an acute solitude, not simply the state of being alone. Cernuda's solitude goes beyond "loneliness" into one of transcendental proportions. He is uniquely alone in an alien universe, a cosmic exile. The poet finds himself ejected from the Eden of his youth, the paradisal garden which is the locus of the child's religious belief. He speaks to solitude in the same way that he will later speak to melancholy in the "Himno a la tristeza."

The opening flourish of the poem immediately announces the theme of the restorative effects of solitude, just as if it were the imagined beloved of the earlier poems. However, this is no longer the projection of amorous desire, nor the remembrance of it, but a total abandonment of earthly love so that solitude itself, paradoxically enough, might accompany the poet:

> Cómo llenarte, soledad,
> Sino contigo misma.

> De niño, entre las pobres guaridas de la tierra,
> Quieto en ángulo oscuro,
> Buscaba en ti, encendida guirnalda,
> Mis auroras futuras y furtivos nocturnos,
> Y en ti los vislumbraba,
> Naturales y exactos, también libres y fieles,
> A semejanza mía,
> A semejanza tuya, eterna soledad.

It is a curious moment in the poetry of Cernuda, for even though the theme of love has been a constant, it has always manifested itself as *unrealized* love, in various states of vicarious or anticipated joy. It may be spurred by seeing it in others, by conjuring it by a simple statement of desire for the "other," or by a studied recalling of it through the memory, giving the poetry an elegiac and nostalgic temper. In the present poem, however, all this is brushed aside as if it were an aberration. The state of solitude is recognized by the poet as his final destiny, the ultimate truth which will always describe his existence on earth. He states that he has wandered through the world seeking an "other" which would deny this, but he has found none, in spite of the enormous appetite for anticipation and remembrance of love. The foregoing is essentially the burden of thought of the following strophe:

> Quería una verdad que a ti te traicionase,
> Olvidando en mi afán
> Cómo las alas fugitivas su propia nube crean.
> ... ...
> Te negué por bien poco;
> Por menudos amores ni ciertos ni fingidos,
> Por quietas amistades de sillón y de gesto,
> Por un nombre de reducida cola en un mundo fantasma
> Por los viejos placeres prohibidos...

The requisite "finding of the self" is ascribed to the introspective powers gained in solitude, not to any human relation:

> Por ti me encuentro ahora, constelados hallazgos,
> Limpios de otro deseo,
> El sol, mi dios, la noche rumorosa,
> La lluvia, intimidad de siempre,
> El bosque y su alentar pagano,
> El mar, el mar como su nombre hermoso;

Solitude embodies itself, becoming the "other":

> Y sobre todos ellos,
> Cuerpo oscuro y esbelto,
> Te encuentro a ti, tú, soledad tan mía,
> Y tú me das fuerza y debilidad
> Como al ave cansada los brazos de la piedra.

The final resolution of the desire for communion with Nature or the "other" is achieved by the healing power of solitude: the poet can vicariously love the multitude and disdain the individual:

> Y así lejos de ellos,
> Ya olvidados sus nombres, los amo en muchedumbres,
> ... ...
> Tú, verdad solitaria,
> Transparente pasión, mi soledad de siempre,
> Eres inmenso abrazo;
> El sol, el mar,
> La oscuridad, la estepa,
> El hombre y su deseo,
> La airada muchedumbre,
> ¿Qué son sino tú misma?

> Por ti, mi soledad los busqué un día;
> En ti, mi soledad, los amo ahora.

> (*RD.*, pp. 106-108.)

This poem marks the final stage in the search for the "other" in the early poetry; it not only completes the alienation and estrangement of the poet from reality and humanity, but it replaces (only temporarily) this impulse to project the self into the "other" with a simple contentment with the state of solitude. Alone in the universe, the poet remains at a distance from the restorative effects of Nature and a belief in an other-worldly existence beyond death. Herein lies the significance of the poem, but this does not mean that the figure of the "other" disappears from the poetry henceforth. His contentment with solitude is a provisional solution to the problem of going beyond the self and reaching the "other." The state is an intolerable one: somehow it must be peopled. The poet continues to make myriad uses of the "other," but these generally appear through the use of the *tú;* that is, a one sided dialogue where only the poet speaks to the "other." Through it, the poet can direct his voice to *someone,* sense another presence. In turn, this desire to speak forces the stylistic ideal to be a colloquial one, without ornament.

The vanquishing of solitude always demands that a word be spoken to an "other." A perfect measure of Cernuda's consistent urge to speak is the poem in the same book which contrasts so distinctly with the resignation and passivity before the world in the "Soliloquio del farero." This poem, "La gloria del poeta," is structured as a completely one-sided exchange of view with a created "other" which takes the form this time of a devil. There was a previous example of the appearance of the devil in the poetry of Cernuda: "Noche del hombre y su demonio," which is considerably later in date than this poem. As we noted in the analysis of the former poem, Cernuda's idea of the devil is not only rooted in Baudelaire's, but also in the demonic impulse cited so often by Goethe. As Cernuda will state in this poem, "somos chispas de un mismo fuego / Y un mismo soplo nos lanzó sobre las ondas tenebrosas / de una extraña creación..." For Cernuda, the devil represents not only the force within him that drives him to write but also the acute critical faculty which reveals the world to him just as it is, with no illusions. By observing other men, the poet confirms that he alone brings to fruition the highest potential of man, while the others simply remain content with themselves and their station, asking nothing further of themselves.

It is difficult to define the substance of this devil, for the poem is a monologue by the poet. Even though the devil is not clearly drawn, there can be no question that the devil is a metaphor for the diabolic vision of the poet. The satanic and amoral figure represents the poet among common men, the creative mind among a conformist and complacent middle class:

Demonio hermano mío, mi semejante,
Te vi palidecer, colgado como la luna matinal,
Oculto en una nube por el cielo,
Entre las horribles montañas,
Una llama a guisa de flor tras la menuda oreja tentadora,
Blasfemando lleno de dicha ignorante,
Igual que un niño cuando entona su plegaria,
Y burlándote cruelmente al contemplar mi cansancio de la tierra.

The poet, after introducing the spectral figure of the devil, his "other," now asks him to view the spectacle of civilized humanity: the ordering and organization of love through "legal" marriage, the intolerable regimentation imposed through the "work week," the codification of beauty by pedants, the explication of the poet's own poetry by the *solemne erudito*. This chaotic enumeration is not at all exhaustive or inclusive, but it is enough to repel the poet, since all these elements work toward negation and the death of the spirit. Let us examine this catalogue of humanity, so to understand better the reasons for the poet's final beseeching of his devil:

Los hombres tú los conoces, hermano mío;
Mírales cómo enderezan su invisible corona
Mientras se borran en la sombra con sus mujeres al brazo,
... ...

Los hijos conseguidos en unos minutos que se hurtaron al sueño
Para dedicarlos a la cohabitación, en la densa tiniebla conyugal
De sus cubiles, escalonados los unos sobre los otros.
... ...

Mira cómo desertan de su trabajo el séptimo día autorizado,
Mientras la caja, el mostrador, la clínica, el bufete, el despacho
[oficial
Dejan pasar el aire con callado rumor por su ámbito solitario.
... ...

Escúchales brotar interminables palabras
Aromatizadas de facilidad violenta,
... ...

Oye sus marmóreos preceptos
Sobre lo útil, lo normal y lo hermoso;
Óyeles dictar la ley al mundo, acotar el amor, dar canon a la
[belleza inexpresable,
Mientras deleitan sus sentidos con altavoces delirantes;

To all this the poet concludes, "Ésos son, hermano mío, / Los seres con quienes muero a solas." This solitude among men remains constant, the poet still unique among men, totally and ontologically alone.

The transcendence of solitude remains the essential problem for the poet: how can he continue to exist in a state of total aloneness? In the poem "Veía sentado," the poet described the union of the image in the pool with the original image in the following way:

> Veía al inclinarme sobre la verdad
> Un cuerpo que no era el cuerpo mío.
>
> Subiendo hasta mí mismo
> Aquí vive desde entonces,
> Mientras aguardo que tu propia presencia
> Haga inútil ese triste trabajo
> De ser yo solo el amor y su imagen.
>
> (*RD.*, pp. 82-83.)

The union so described is only a temporary victory over solitude — the *real* presence of the "other" is still sought by the poet. The fact that the poet describes only a temporary resolution of the problem is of little importance; this is one of the means with which the poet tries to overcome his detachment from humanity.

Exactly the same desire for union with the created "other" takes place in this poem. The upward movement of the image in the pool into the body of the poet is now replaced by more overtly sexual imagery. The devil becomes the lover and mistress of the poet, and the resultant union gives him the same imperious and "diabolic" stance before the world exemplified in the devil himself. In the following strophes, the poet speaks to the devil:

> Sabes sin embargo que mi voz es la tuya,
> Que mi amor es el tuyo;
> Deja, oh, deja por una larga noche
> Resbalar tu cálido cuerpo oscuro,
> Ligero como un látigo,
> Bajo el mío, momia de hastío sepulta en anónima yacija,
> Y que tus besos, ese venero inagotable,
> Viertan en mí la fiebre de una pasión a muerte entre los dos;
> ... ...
> Es hora ya, es más que tiempo
> De que tus manos cedan a mi vida
> El amargo puñal codiciado del poeta;
> De que lo hundas, con sólo un golpe limpio,
> En este pecho sonoro y vibrante, idéntico a un laúd,
> Donde la muerte únicamente,
> La muerte únicamente,
> Puede hacer resonar la melodía prometida.
>
> (*RD.*, pp. 113-115.)

The metaphorical description of the sexual act depicts all the more starkly the character of the poet's supplication to his diabolical muse. In place of the rather bland upward movement of the reflection seen in the pool into the poet himself, the passionate desire of the poet for union is here expressed as sexual lust.

In our brief examination of the figure of the "other" in the poetry of Cernuda, we came to certain conclusions which it would be best to repeat here, for we are about to enter a new phase in the poetry, and a reiteration of the material covered so far is essential if we are to continue our investigation with a full knowledge of what has gone before. After establishing the existence of the *interior hombre*, we found that the created "other" took two forms in the early poetry: one as the imagined companion or lover, having an essentially sentimental or amorous basis. As an example of this, we spoke of the Narcissistic aspects of such a poem as "Estaba tendido," where the poet frankly states that the lover beside him is a figment of his own imagination. As the polar opposite of this technique, we cited the use of the *tú*, where the poet spoke to himself as if he were an "other." As examples of this kind of division of the self, we cited the poems "De qué país," and "Sentado sobre un golfo de sombra," where the poet did not make use of a created "other," but rather remained within, so to speak, and let his *interior hombre* speak to him.

In our chronological survey of the problem, we found that the two techniques more often than not fused into one. The imaginative presence of the "other" was physically engulfed by the poet himself. In the poem "Veía sentado," the image in the pool rose and became one with the poet. In "Mi Arcángel," and the "Soliloquio del farero," we analyzed two distinct characters: the archangel and the personification of solitude. The common ground among the two is shared by their total identity with the poet, for both the angel and the figure of solitude are irrevocably bound to the poet. The union of the "other" with the *interior hombre* took on all the aspects of a physical union between humans in the poem just analyzed, "La gloria del poeta."

The poems that follow are precisely those that formed the basis for the first chapters of this book: "Himno a la tristeza" and "A las estatuas de los dioses." These poems, it will be remembered, introduced us to the long series of elegies which are the hallmark of the book that follows "Invocaciones," *Las nubes*. In the latter book, which contains almost no examples of the imagined "other," we find instead actual physical presences that replace what was only imagined formerly. For example, we have the elegiac "Noche de luna," two "Elegía(s) Española(s)," a poem entitled "Niño muerto," the beginnings of dramatic poetry in "Resaca en San-sueña," "La adoración de los Magos," and "Lázaro," and finally the meditative poetry that is "Violetas" and "Ruiseñor sobre la piedra." Although this is hardly a comprehensive description of the contents of the book, I hope that it is sufficient to show that the poet, under the emotional charge of the Spanish Civil War and the resultant exile in England, felt no need to address a figment of the imagination. Too many objects had been forced upon him already by the reality around him: the dead Lorca, vanquished Spain, a child's death during wartime, and finally an appeal to the Divinity as exemplified in "La visita de Dios," "Atardecer en la catedral," and "La adoración de los Magos."

However, with the final realization by the poet that a return to his homeland was impossible, and that exile in an alien environment was to be his sole existence for an indeterminate amount of time, there is a gradual reappearance of imagined objects. Instead of experience in reality imposing itself on the poetry, it becomes increasingly a dialogue within the mind, disembodied, as it were, from the world that surrounds the poet. With this new and welcome appearance of imaginary figures which serve as the focus in the poetry, the "other" now appears with definite existential overtones, most evident in the later poems from the period just after the end of the Second World War.

Before commenting upon these poems, it would be best to examine the four kinds of poems directed to the "other" that we shall encounter in Cernuda's poetry after *Las nubes*. The most common use, and the one with which we are already familiar through our examination of earlier poems, is that of the *interior hombre* speaking to the poet, serving as a moral foil to the desires and the human impulses of the poet. The second type is that of the poet speaking to an imaginary lover, a technique already familiar to us from the earlier poems. The third type encompasses those poems which center around the poet and his poetry: the most interesting of these are "A un poeta futuro," where the poet speaks to a poet not yet born, and "Apologia pro Vita Sua," where the poet, in a perfect instance of *desdoblamiento*, imagines himself to be a dying man, inviting all his acquaintances around his deathbed to view the spectacle of the moribund poet. We shall also analyze three poems treating of the "double" of the poet: "El poeta," "Retrato de poeta," and "La poesía." The fourth type, and by far the most complex, is found in the book, *Vivir sin estar viviendo,* which contains poems documenting a total and unalterable division within the self. These poems begin with "El intruso," and end with the very late "Viendo volver," a culminating point in the technique of the "other" in the poetry of Cernuda.

The *tú* is another means that the poet employs from the perspective of the *interior hombre* to speak to himself without having recourse to the imaginary "other." An example of this self-address in the late poetry is "Aplauso humano," which documents the heroic fidelity to the spirit of poetry that has always characterized Cernuda. It is not a selfless and unmotivated devotion, however; the poet has a clear goal to which he aspires: immortality through the poetic word. He contrasts this with the mundane tasks of ordinary life, destined only for sensual gratification or self-preservation. The poet on the other hand, while not completely free from the constrictions that are inherent in any human, does at least attempt to base his life upon something else than a rampant desire for pleasure and money. In Cernuda's terms, those numberless masses who exemplify "l'homme moyen sensuel" are nothing but "aquellas criaturas grises":

> Ahora todas aquellas criaturas grises
> Cuya sed parca de amor nocturnamente satisface
> El aguachirle conyugal, al escuchar tus versos,
> Por la verdad que exponen podrán escarnecerte.
>
> Cuánto pedante en moda y periodista en venta
> Humana flor perfecta se estimarán entonces
> Frente a ti, así como el patán rudimentario
> Hasta la náusea hozando la escoria del deseo.

This poem, "Aplauso humano," opens with this violent contrast between the sexual act ordained by society and the unordered and socially superflous act of writing poetry. The speaker here takes on a complimentary and approving tone toward the work of the poet; after all, it is the inner conscience of the poet that speaks to him in this way. Poetry is here glorified in opposition to serving a State or a Religion:

> La consideración mundana tú nunca la buscaste,
> Aún menos cuando fuera su precio una mentira,
> Como bufón sombrío traicionando tu alma
> A cambio de un cumplido con oficial benevolencia.
>
> Por ello en vida y muerte pagarás largamente
> La ocasión de ser fiel contigo y unos pocos,
> Aunque jamás sepan los otros que desvío
> Siempre es razón mejor ante la grey.

The solitude of the poet among the crowd, the complete separation that he demands for himself in the world can only lead to him speaking to himself, encouraging his own spirit to continue on the road before him, not to lead into vain causes and spurious religious belief. The life of man alone, Cernuda maintains, is not an easy one, but it is the unique path to follow if the individual is to remain faithful to his poetic gift. Poetry is a self-sufficient and uniquely justifiable exercise of the human spirit, needing no alliance to the State or to a Religion for it to be viable, valid and great. Cernuda insists, not without traces of paranoia, that the society revenges itself upon the poet for not taking up its banner. The poet cannot take part in society: solitude is the unique state for the man who seeks truth.

> Pero a veces aún dudas si la verdad del alma
> No debiera guardarla el alma a solas,
> Contemplarla en silencio, y así nutrir la vida
> Con un tesoro intacto que no profana el mundo.
>
> Mas tus labios hablaron, y su verdad fue al aire.
> Sigue con la frente tranquila entre los hombres,
> Y si un sarcasmo escuchas, súbito como piedra,
> Formas amargas del elogio ahí descifre tu orgullo.

> (RD., pp. 216-217.)

The final point for the poet is a simple sense of dignity and self-justification that wins over the impulse to serve and "be useful." Like the majority of the poets of his generation, the alliance to causes, even during the trial by fire that was the Spanish Civil War, was sporadic and short-lived. The poet's demonic ability to turn aside error and seek truth soon taught him how fruitless it was to find a justification for existence outside the self. It is only within, in dialogue with the *interior hombre*, can life be made valid and meaningful.

In a later poem from the same book, "Como quien espera el alba," the poet carries the process of the divorcement from the world one step further: the whole mechanism of life is put into question. Even though the justification for the self is now resolutely based upon the inner man, the poet himself cannot entirely disregard what he sees around him. The land in which he was born is now alien to him, his friends distant or dead.

The voice that speaks to the poet is now a cautious and didactic one, in contrast to the complimentary tone of the previous poem. This voice instructs the poet about the vanity of the world, and urges him to disdain the endless changes that occur in Nature, himself and the world every day:

> Nuestra vida parece que está aquí: con hojas
> Seguras en su rama, hasta quen nazca el frío;
> Con flores en su tallo, hasta que brote el viento;
> Con luz allá en su cielo, hasta que surjan nubes.
> Tal vez por un momento cierto te creyeras
> En el mundo del hombre, si no fuese
> Por aquel otro mundo de las sombras
> Que al cuerpo lo consume como a luna menguante.

Indeed, the voice of the inner man has changed: the tone of foreboding and immanence still leads the "other" to the same conclusions: a contentment with the self, a quiescent silence should reign over us so that we might savor experience to the fullest. With this premonition of death seen in the mutability of all Nature, the inner voice preaches acceptance of what is surely to come:

> ¿Qué empresa nuestra es ésta, abandonada
> Inútilmente un día? ¿Qué afectos imperiosos

Éstos, con cuyos nombres se alimenta el olvido?
Ya en tu vida las sombras pesan más que los cuerpos;
Llámalos hoy, si hay alguno que escuche
Entre la hierba sola de esta primavera,
Y aprende ese silencio antes que el tiempo llegue.

(RD., pp. 219-220.)

The third and last poem of the first group, typifying the use of the *interior hombre,* is "Vereda del cuco," which also will introduce us to the second group of poems, those where the poet speaks to an inexistent being. This particular poem is singularly difficult to analyze, if it can be done at all, for it is a perfect summation of some of the most salient characteristics of Cernuda's search for love. Phillip Silver sees it as a formulation of the twofold evolution of love, mortal and divine, which in turn bespeaks both a thirst for eternity and a need for human love. The symbol for this is the fountain, which incites and quenches this thirst at the same time. The love for adolescents is seen as a love for the poet's own youth, a Narcissism extended beyond the self so that it might reincarnate itself in others.

How does the poet use this inner voice to project his experience, dramatize it, and make it knowable to the reader? The symbolic intent of the fountain is immediately evident: the poet sees himself reflected in the pool, his "other" which remains, in spite of the fact that the water is active and dynamic, symbolic of the passing time:

> Cuántas veces has ido en otro tiempo
> Camino de esta fuente,
> Buscando por la senda oscura
> Adonde mana el agua,
> Para quedar inmóvil en su orilla,
> Mirando con asombro mudo
> Cómo allá, entre la hondura,
> Con gesto semejante aunque remoto,
> Surgía otra apariencia
> De encanto ineludible,
> Propicia y enemiga,
> Y tú la contemplabas,
> Como aquel que contempla
> Revelarse el destino
> Sobre la arena en signos inconstantes.

Love, then, begins with self-love, an adulation of one's own image in the pool. This reflection awakens a desire for an "other." The sight of the reflection does not quench the desire, but aggravates it:

> ...bebiste del agua
> Tornándose tu sed luego más viva...

The initial contact with the image is simply that of egocentric self-love, but it foreshadows other forms of love. In taking water from the fountain, the poet identifies with the water there at that instant: it changes, the image does not.

> Y al invocar la hondura
> Una imagen distinta respondía,
> Evasiva a la mente,
> Ofreciendo, escondiendo
> La expresión inmutable,
> La compañía fiel en cuerpos sucesivos
> Que el amor es lo eterno y no lo amado.

The poet seeks the gift of love, but not its bringer. As we saw in "Veía sentado" and "La gloria del poeta," the desired object was the image of the "other," whether it was a reflection in the pool or an imagined devil. But in fact, this object was nothing but another entity which evoked the Narcissism of the poet. The union of the image in the pool with the self, the descent of the devil into the poet's body is here repeated in a different way, for the adolescents that the poet sees around him are now conclusively defined as objects in which the poet can recreate his own youth:

> Como flor encendidas,
> Como el aire ligeras,
> Mira esas otras formas juveniles
> Bajo las ramas donde silba el cuco,
> Que invocan hoy la imagen
> Oculta allá en la fuente,
> Como tú ayer; y dudas si no eres
> Su sed hoy nueva, si no es tu amor el suyo,
> En ellos redivivo, ...

The distance in time is irrelevant here. The poet realizes that these "others" are substitutes for his own reflection:

> Aunque tu día haya pasado,
> Eres tú, y son los idos,
> Quienes por estos ojos nuevos buscan
> En la haz de la fuente
> La realidad profunda,
> Íntima y perdurable;
> Eres tú, y son los idos,
> Quienes por estos cuerpos nuevos vuelven
> A la vereda oscura,
> Y ante el tránsito ciego de la noche
> Huyen hacia el oriente,
> Dueños del sortilegio,
> Conocedores del fuego originario,
> La pira donde el fénix muere y nace.

> (*RD.*, pp. 229-232.)

Beginning with the initial and rather regretful tone with which the inner voice addresses the poet, we arrive at the true meaning of the image in the pool: self-love is the first manifestation of a love for an "other." It is not superseded even when the poet disdains his own image and seeks it in others. The effect still remains the same, for love restores again his own youth and halts the passage of time. For Cernuda, revealed love is truth. Consequently, the poem ends in affirmation and acceptance, in contrast with the reproachful tone of recrimination with which it opened. For this reason, the poet not only makes use of the inner voice, but also of a projected voice to a non-existent being.

In the poems "Amando en el tiempo" and "Cuatro poemas a una sombra," the technique of the "other" is carried one step further. A greater distance between the poet and the "other" becomes apparent, for it is impossible to link the imagined figure to a simple reflection of the self. The evidence contained in these poems indicates an "other" which is distinct from the poet, not a representation of his image, nor a product of the "desdoblamiento del yo."

"Amando en el tiempo" begins with the *tú* form of address, but this alters rapidly, for the "other" has no relation to the poet. The poem documents the undermining power of time over the minds and bodies of men. They still sense the impulse to love, but are agonizingly aware of time's deleterious effects upon themselves and those they love:

> El tiempo, insinuándose en tu cuerpo,
> Como nube de polvo en fuente pura,
> Aquella gracia antigua desordena
> Y clava en mí una pena silenciosa.

The fact that this is only the inevitable wearing-away of time is of no consolation to the poet, for the lessons learned by our ancestors must be relearned and suffered again:

> Otros antes que yo vieron un día,
> Y otros luego verán, cómo decae
> La amada forma esbelta, recordando
> De cuánta gloria es cifra un cuerpo hermoso.
>
> Pero la vida solos la aprendemos,
> Y placer y dolor se ofrecen siempre
> Tal mundo virgen para cada hombre;
> Así mi pena inculta es nueva ahora.
>
> Nueva como lo fuese al primer hombre,
> Que cayó con su amor del paraíso,
> Cuando viera, su cielo ya vencido
> Por sombras, decaer el cuerpo amado.
>
> (*RD.*, p. 225.)

The *tú* form which was employed in the first strophe disappears, and the poem continues without any personal reference to the end, indicating all the more clearly that the "other" imagined in this kind of poem is illusory and imaginative, a product of the poet's drive toward it. As the poet stated in "Vereda del cuco," "... el amor es lo eterno y no lo amado," but the love itself cannot be considered as such without another being who is conscious of being loved and who corresponds. This being so, the poet abstracts the beloved, drains him of any warmth or animation, making an "other" a disengaged and bloodless entity.

The "Cuatro poemas a una sombra" are important not only for the additional light which they throw upon Cernuda's theory of love, but also for the way in which the imagined presence of the beloved ends by comforting the poet. The "other" makes the poet's own identity more real and viable to himself, helping him to establish or renew a network of relationships from which he has been alienated by his own temperamental disposition.

> Recuerda la ventana
> Sobre el jardín nocturno,
> Casi conventual; aquel sonido humano,
> Oscuro de las hojas, cuando el tiempo,
> Lleno de la presencia y la figura amada,
> Sobre la eternidad un ala inmóvil,
> Hace ya de tu vida
> Centro cordial del mundo,
> De ti puesto en olvido,
> Enajenado entre las cosas.

The poet defines himself and the reality around him through the medium of the imagined figure. In a later stanza, this is made more vivid: "Cuando por el amor tu espíritu rescata / La realidad profunda." The figure of the "other" as we defined it in the first section of this chapter, brings with it a total sense of plenitude and fulfillment which solitude, in spite of the many efforts of the poet to make of it what it is not, cannot bestow upon men. It is precisely this sense of "being alive" which the "other" brings:

> Sin esperarle, contra el tiempo,
> Nuevamente ha venido,
> Rompiendo el sueño largo
> Por cuyo despertar te aparecía
> La muerte sólo; y trae
> El sentido consigo, la pasión, la conciencia,
> Como recién creados admirables,
> En su pureza y su vigor primeros,
> Que estando ya, no estaban,
> Pues entre estar y estar hay diferencia.

The difference is, of course, in whether one is accompanied through life or simply alone, without contact with an "other." If this contact were to take place, the defensive ego of the self would give way gladly to a sense of sharing, a more pliant and less combative individuality. In this poem, he gladly accepts the demands which the "other" makes upon him, even though its identity remains "aún desconocido."

El amor nace en los ojos,
Adonde tú, perdidamente,
Tiemblas de hallarle aún desconocido,
Sonriente, exigiendo;
La mirada es quien crea,
Por el amor, el mundo,
Y el amor quien percibe,
Dentro del hombre oscuro, el ser divino,
Criatura de luz entonces viva
En los ojos que ven y que comprenden.

The twofold nature of love is thus mortal *and* divine. The whole series of poems that we are now analyzing should not be read with *eros* in mind, but rather a fusion of the latter with *agape*, the platonic ideal. Love remains incomplete and fruitless if not complemented by the "other":

El dios y el hombre unirlos:
En obras de la tierra lo divino olvidado,
Lo terreno probado en el fuego celeste...

(*RD.*, pp. 235-237.)

The poem which follows "La ventana" is entitled "El amigo," and it formulates again the curious interplay between the imagined "other" and the image of the poet himself as reflected in the pool or in the youth he observes. Many times the envisioned "other" becomes "one" with the poet, appearing to him while alone, a willful contrivance to people the barren mental landscape that is his. "El amigo" is one of the clearest formulations of Cernuda's attempt to break beyond the bonds of solitude by means of a feigned state of attachment to an "other." The majority of Cernuda's poems rarely depict the poet in contact with the "other" in the present, usually anticipating its presence or recalling it through memory. In "El amigo," the effect is here nostalgic:

Los lugares idénticos parecen,
Las cosas como antes,
Mas él no está, ni la luz, ni las hojas,
Y en esta calma hacia el final del año
Llevas la soledad por toda compañía.

The image of absence is summed up by the poet's shadow, the only thing which accompanies him now. While viewing it, the poet esteems it as an "other," that is to say, his mind turns irrevocably toward a state of union with an "other" in the past:

> Es grato errar afuera,
> Ir con tu sombra, recordando
> Lo pasado tan cerca en lo presente,
> Crecida ya su flor sin tiempo.
> ¿Es ésta soledad si así está llena?
> ... ...
>
> En su sosiego crees
> Que una forma ligera se encamina
> Dulcemente a tu lado,
> Como el amigo aquel, cuando las hojas
> Y la luz, luego idas con él mismo.

However, this is not an irremediable alienation. The remembered "other" unites with the poet, the loved one becomes a reflection of the physical attributes of the poet himself. The union brought about between the self and the "other" in this poem is relatively complex, for the poet first professes nothing but a common identity of lives:

> Le llamas ido, y no semeja
> Su vida, transcurriendo a la distancia,
> Espectro de la mente hoy,
> Sino vida en la tuya, entre estas cosas
> Que le vieron contigo.

The identity becomes more intense as the poet realizes that the "other" is a part of him. What was a juxtaposition becomes a union:

> Negado a tu deseo, hallas entonces
> Que si tocas tu mano es con su mano,
> Que si miran tus ojos es con sus ojos,
> Y tu amor en ti mismo
> Tiene cuanto le dio y en él perdiera.

The last strophe depicts even more than a union — it is a oneness and identity between the two, negating the duality with which the poem began. The beloved becomes the poet himself, *Narcissus redivivus:*

No le busques afuera. Él ya no puede
Ser distinto de ti, ni tú tampoco
Ser distinto de él; unidos vais,
Formando un solo ser de dos impulsos,
Como al pájaro solo hacen dos alas.

(*RD.*, pp.. 237-238.)

The final strophe of the fourth poem is even more explicit:

Junto al agua, en la hierba, ya no busques,
Que no hallarás figura, sino allá en la mente
Continuarse el mito de tu existir aún incompleto,
Creando otro deseo, dando asombro a la vida,
Sueño de alguno donde tú no sabes.

(*RD.*, p. 241.)

In the third category, the poet finally becomes the "other";
many of these poems have as their subject the topic of poetry
itself. The poet either envisions a poet not yet born or himself
as moribund, or even explains his poetics through the figure of
the poet in such poems as "El poeta," "Retrato de poeta," or "La
poesía."

An interesting example is "A un poeta futuro," where the
poet speaks to a fictional poet not yet born. He is represented in
the poem by the fountain, which has always signified for Cernuda
all that is promise: latent, unfulfilled, and undisciplined energy.
The life which the future poet must live is symbolized by the river,
that amorphous and incomprehensible mass that drains the fountain of its substance. Death is symbolized, as it was for Manrique,
by the sea: the terminal point for both the fountain and the river,
a fulfillment which is at the same time stillness, paralysis, and
death. At the beginning of the poem, the poet is closer to the sea
than he is to the fountain, but his voice calls to the poet of
the future, and not to death:

No comprendo a los ríos. Con prisa errante pasan
Desde la fuente al mar, en ocio atareado,
Llenos de su importancia, bien fabril o agrícola;
La fuente, que es promesa, el mar sólo la cumple,
El multiforme mar, incierto y sempiterno,
Como en fuente lejana, en el futuro

> Duermen las formas posibles de la vida
> En un sueño de sueños, nulas e inconscientes,
> Prontas a reflejar la idea de los dioses.
> Y entre los seres que serán un día
> Sueñas tu sueño, mi imposible amigo.

The poem develops on an even broader plane: supposing that the time within which men live somehow coincided with the Divine concept of time, an endless continuum wherein man could meet the future and the past. If so, Luis Cernuda and the poet-to-be would become one universal poet, superior to the individuals that have practiced the art of poetry from Homer onwards. Again, the two become one:

> Si el tiempo de los hombres y el tiempo de los dioses
> Fuera uno, esta nota que en mí inaugura el ritmo,
> Unida con la tuya se acordaría en cadencia,
> No callando sin eco entre el mudo auditorio.

Thus the search for the poet-that-does-not-yet-exist finally resolves into another mutation of the eternal search for the "other":

> ... tú no sabrás con cuándo amor hoy busco
> Por ese abismo blanco del tiempo venidero
> La sombra de tu alma, para aprender de ella
> A ordenar mi pasión según nueva medida.

The poet of the future aids the poet in breaking the solitude of his present state. In the future, the solitude of death will be alleviated by a reading of the present poet's poems:

> Yo no podré decirte cuánto llevo luchando
> Para que mi palabra no se muera
> Silenciosa conmigo, y vaya como un eco
> A ti, como tormenta que ha pasado
> Y un són vago recuerda por el aire tranquilo.
> ... ...
> ... presiento en este alejamiento humano
> Cuán míos habrán de ser los hombres venideros,
> Cómo esta soledad será poblada un día,
> Aunque sin mí, de camaradas puros a tu imagen.
> Si renuncio a la vida es para hallarla luego
> Conforme a mi deseo, en tu memoria.

The poet renounces companionship on earth so as to be assured of one throughout eternity, that reader of the future. When the future poet reads the poet of today, the unity of intent will be evident: both deny the world and glorify the art of poetry. The poetry that Cernuda writes will come forth out of the book not as simple words written years before, but rather as prefigurations of the same thoughts and ideas of the future poet — the two will be one again.

> Cuando... lleve el destino
> Tu mano hacia el volumen donde yazcan
> Olvidados mis versos, y lo abras,
> Yo sé que sentirás mi voz llegarte,
> No de la letra vieja, mas del fondo
> Vivo en tu entraña, con un afán sin nombre
> Que tú dominarás. Escúchame y comprende.
> En sus limbos mi alma quizá recuerde algo,
> Y entonces en ti mismo mis sueños y deseos
> Tendrán razón al fin, y habré vivido.

> (*RD*., pp. 200-202).

The idea as similar to Unamuno's, who also believed that his own life was brought to a final justification through the unconscious action of future readers who relive the passions and sentiments of the author. The unity of the self and the "other" (which is a projected existence in the future) is here achieved through the medium of the poetic act, unifying all poets in a common bond of dedication to the art. In any case, we can recognize the similarity of this poem to the others in this series: the poet remains alone, and the poem becomes a means to conquer this state through a union with a being that does not yet exist, but who will ultimately complete the work of the poet now writing the poem.

In a poem that is similar to the foregoing, the poet contemplates a poet on his deathbed, meditating on the final significance of the life he is about to leave. The spirit of Goethe is very much present in the poem, and certainly the final line "para que entre la luz abrid las puertas" is an almost exact translation of Goethe's dying words. [11] It is not important to know whether the figure of the moribund poet is Goethe or not: it is yet another case of an emotional projection of the poet into a dramatic situation or character, The voice is that of the poet who is dying; after an introductory strophe, he invites the bereaved into his room in a telling example of the poet as the imagined "other":

> Dejadles que se acerquen a mi cama
> Y alumbren sus semblantes, como estrellas
> Suspensas en la noche sobre el agua oscura,
> La agonía de aquel que les amara,
> Uniéndoles así, desconocidos los unos a los otros,
> En apretados haces de recuerdos.

The bedroom is in darkness, and the poet clamors for more light, not only for his eyes, but for his spirit. The poet's soul is compared to a bird who has lost the power of flight: "Yo contemplo / La mía, como pájaro herido bajo un ala / Que a tierra viene, mas lucha todavía / Con plumas abolidas que no sostiene el aire." The loss of light and warmth is feared more than death itself: "La renuncia a la luz más que la muerte es dura." The only consolation if it can be termed that, is the final hope of resurrection which the poet hopes for, in spite of his incredulity:

> He vivido sin ti, mi Dios, pues no ayudaste [12]
> Esta incredulidad que hizo triste mi alma.
> Heme aquí ya vencido, presa fácil ahora
> De tus ministros, cuyas manos alzadas
> Remiten o condenan a los actos del hombre.

The decomposition of the body into water, air, fire and earth brings the elements back into Creation in the Heraclitean circle. The dust is the only substance which remains; the poet asks whether it will speak or not: "cuando yo muera, el polvo dirá sus alabanzas? / Quien su verdad declare, será el polvo?" The

---

[11] "Macht doch den Fensterladen im Schlafgemach auf, damit mehr Licht herein komme," as cited in *A New Dictionary of Quotations* (New York, 1946), p. 696.

[12] "Straightaway the father of the child cried out, and said, I believe: help thou mine unbelief." Mark IX: 24.

only relief from the total destruction of the body must be a resurrection of the spirit that parallels in the realm of the spirit the desire for light that the dying poet expresses while still on earth:

> Si dijiste, mi Dios, cómo ninguno
> De los que en ti confíen ha de ser desolado,
> Tras esta noche oscura vendrá el alba
> Y hallaremos en ti resurrección y vida.
> Para que entre la luz abrid las puertas.

> (*RD.*, pp. 204-208).

The group of three poems that now concern us constitutes a final synthesis of the various kinds of poems that Cernuda has written concerning the poet and his art. The first, "El poeta," is a kind of *Ars Poetica* which employs the figure of the poet as the center of attention. The second, "Retrato de poeta," is a poem addressed to the portrait of Fray Hortensio Paravicino by El Greco, now in the Museum of Fine Arts in Boston, where Cernuda viewed it. The third poem, "La poesía," is a marvelously concise characterization of the knid of *servidumbre* to poetry that Cernuda has always sensed within himself. The three poems are written with a common background of artistic accomplishment and a justified pride in it. This faith in his own work is a complete trust in the intangible. With it, the poet sees the essential newness in all things, so that poetry is continually transforming reality to abstraction, and then treated according to the dictates of poetic thought.

The first poem, "El poeta," has a semi-anonymous poet of another generation, surely Bécquer, as its subject. Given the fact that Cernuda's affinity to Bécquer is well known and has been rather exhaustively discussed recently, there is no reason to doubt that the poet referred to is Bécquer himself. The first strophe documents the effect of that poet's work upon the young Cernuda:

> La edad tienes ahora que él entonces,
> Cuando en el tiempo de la siembra y la danza,
> Hijos de anhelo moceril que se despierta,
> Tu sueño, tu esperanza, tu secreto,
> Aquellos versos fueron a sus manos
> Para mostrar y hallar signo de vida.

This "sign of life" is to be recurrent in the poetry of Cernuda, for he has continually emphasized the function of poetry in his life as the only justification for his existence. The spiritual antecedent of Cernuda knew this reverence for poetry in spite of a chaotic and disordered life. He knew too that the simple contemplation of things was the key to the poetical experience:

> Con reverencia y con amor así aprendiste,
> Aunque en torno los hombres no curen de la imagen
> Misteriosa y divina de las cosas,
> De él, a mirar quieto, como
> Espejo, sin el cual la creación sería
> Ciega, hasta hallar su mirada en el poeta.

In a sense, we are in the presence of another spiritual double of the poet, an "other" who, generations before, underwent almost the same spiritual crises that the poet Cernuda experienced. As we have noted in our analyses of the "other," the figure tends to unite with the poet: in this particular poem, this occurs again.

> Aquel tiempo pasó, o tú pasaste,
> Agitando una estela temporal ilusoria,
> Adonde estaba él, cuando tenía
> La misma edad que hoy tienes:
> Lo que su fe sabía y la tuya buscaba,
> Ahora has encontrado.

This companionship which Cernuda senses with a poet from his own native city relieves the inevitable solitude:

> Agradécelo pues, que una palabra
> Amiga mucho vale
> En nuestra soledad, en nuestro breve espacio
> De vivos, y nadie sino tú puede decirle,
> A aquel que te enseñara adónde y cómo crece:
> Gracias por la rosa del mundo.

The medium of poetry is recognized for what it is — a way to unify experience from among varying spatial and temporal planes:

> Para el poeta hallarla es lo bastante,
> E inútil el renombre u olvido de su obra,
> Cuando en ella un momento se unifican,

Tal uno son amante, amor y amado,
Los tres complementarios luego y antes dispersos:
El deseo, la rosa y la mirada.

(*RD.*, pp. 251-253.)

In the same way, the poem dedicated to Fray Hortensio Paravicino describes this unifying effect achieved by poetry as a real
manifestation of a faith in the world of the spirit: "Esta palabra ...
la recuerda / Cómo va nuestra fe hacia las cosas / Ya no vistas
afuera con los ojos." The contemplation of Nature that was
advocated in the previous poem is here exemplified by the lan-
gorous and passive expression of Fray Hortensio. Before, this was
termed "mirar quieto," but now the preacher-poet looks out upon
"... Las cosas mismas que sostienen tu vida, / Como la tierra
aquella, sus encinas, sus rocas, / Que estás ahí mirando quieta-
mente."

Both Cernuda and Paravicino find themselves in this state
of isolation from humanity, a limbo that all poets are destined to
haunt while on earth. Both find themselves fallen from an original
state of divine beings. Is a life in poetry enough, or must art be
abandoned so that life may be lived more fully? Cernuda feels
sure that in Fray Hortensio's case, life had no quarrel with art.
But in his own situation, he finds a division within himself on
this point, a topic which will be more fully explored in a later
poem. Here, it is presented to us *in nuce:*

>   ... Tú viviste tu día,
> Y en él, con otra vida que el pintor te infunde,
> Existes hoy. Yo ¿estoy viviendo el mío?

The conflict between man's appetite for experience and the
ascetic cast that the poet professes for art is more clearly dramatized in the poem "La poesía," where each of the stanzas
represents the poet at a different age and consequently a different attitude toward poetry:

>   Para tu siervo el sino le escogiera,
>   Y absorto y entregado, el niño
>   ¿Qué podía hacer sino seguirte?

El mozo luego, enamorado, conocía
Tu poder sobre él, y lo ha servido
Como a nada en la vida, contra todo.

Pero el hombre algún día, al preguntarse:
La servidumbre larga qué le ha deparado,
Su libertad envidió a uno, otro su fortuna.

Y quiso ser él mismo, no servirte
Más, y vivir para sí, entre los hombres.
Tú le dejaste, como a un niño, a su capricho.

Poetry demands that the poet be other than he is, and precisely this "schizophrenic" tendency in the practice of art is the burden of the poet's complaint. This poem affords us a final key to the interpretation of the continual sense of "otherness" that is present in Cernuda's use of the subject of poetry as a topic for a poem. Artistic creation demands that the personal experience of the artist be sometimes transcended. But this has its dangers. In the case of Unamuno, the divergence between the self as seen from the public point of view and the *real* one came to signify a harrowing impasse for him, since he saw himself not as a real person, but as a creature that existed more as a manifestation of art than a man of flesh and bones. His life became a springboard for his work, not an end in itself. We can well understand in this regard the terror that Unamuno felt when a madman in Barcelona inquired of him, "Es usted el auténtico?"

This poem by Cernuda is by no means as extreme a manifestation of this *asco de sí como artista,* but there can be no doubt that the divergence of the self that poetry demands has been keenly felt by the poet. The desire to be oneself and to live for oneself (vivir para sí) is a tacit recognition that life is not art, and that one must be served and the other neglected. This poem ends by reaffirming in a conventional way the superiority of art over life, despite the well-founded doubts that the poet suggests to himself in the previous stanzas:

Pero después, pobre sin ti de todo,
A tu voz que llamaba, o al sueño de ella,
Vivo en su servidumbre respondió: "Señora".

(*RD.,* pp. 298-299.)

The final set of poems are by far the most complex, for they document the division of the self. They are disconcerting, for they introduce us to a world of disorientation and doubt where all safe guides and all faith have been discarded, and the being continues through life hounded by the presence of the "other" within him, this alien and extraneous creature. As a typical example of the duplication of the self into the figure of the "other," there is the poem "El intruso," a revealing instance of the bedevilment of the self by the "other": the poet imagines himself as *not* himself, living the life of another in another age:

> Como si equivocara el tiempo
> Su trama de los días,
> Vives acaso los de otro?
> Extrañas ya la vida.

His is not a fear of reincarnation. Rather, he senses himself as not living his own life, unconvinced of his own existence. His essential and real self remains unlived and in potential, while an extraneous and irrelevant being occupies his body, using it, sapping it of energies that should rightly be expended by the true self. The alienation of the self with the "other" is summed up in the last line, "extrañas ya la vida," signalling that the life lived by the poet is not his own, but is of another. The distance between the "other" and the self is both spatial and temporal:

> Lejos de ti, de la conciencia
> Desacordada, el centro
> Buscas afuera, entre las cosas
> Presentes un momento.

The self, due to the impulse toward the eternal and a revulsion against death, tries to seek a more permanent and immovable base, as it were, for his life. The poet falls into the fetish of things, having lost the assurance of his own identity. This reorientation takes the form of a transfiguration of the mortal self into an "other." It defines the disordered self, anchors it in a strong bond. But if the "other" is illusory and disembodied, it can orient the self only haphazardly:

> Así de aquel amigo joven
> Que fuiste ayer, aguardas
> En vano ante el umbral de un sueño
> La ilusa confianza.

The effort is delusionary and futile, a hopeless attempt to escape from the sentient self. The shock of recognition is administered by the poet's image of himself in the mirror:

> Pero tu faz, en el alinde
> De algún espejo, vieja,
> Hosca abstraída, te interrumpe
> Tal la presencia ajena.

The frightening possibility that the "other" is more authentic than the real self now becomes the obsessive theme of the poem. The figure that speaks the poem has no right to do so or to act in the world, for he is a feigned shadow for the authentic, which is the "other" — the self broken into selves by a cracked mirror. We can see that in this hallucinatory play of perspectives, the viability of the self has been completely eradicated:

> Hoy este intruso eres tú mismo,
> Tú, como el otro antes,
> Y con el cual sin gusto inicias
> Costumbre a que se allane.

> Para llegar al que no eres,
> Quien no eres te guía,
> Cuando el amigo es el extraño
> Y la rosa es la espina.
>
> (RD., pp. 241-242.)

The sense of the "other" is radically altered: the self has no substance and is threatened with engulfment by the "other," to the extent that the "other" directs the helpless and pliant self.

The search for authenticity does not especially require the "other". In the poem "El retraído," the problem is envisioned in terms of various degrees of life "genuineness." Here, the poet wishes to live a life that is less alien to himself than the one he now lives:

Vivir contigo quieres
Vida menos ajena que esta otra,
Donde placer y pena
No sean accidentes encontrados,
Sino faces del alma
Que refleja el destino
Con la fidelidad trasmutadora
De la imagen brotando en aguas quietas.

(*RD.*, p. 248.)

The unification with the "other" is carried to an extreme in the
poem "El éxtasis," where the poet becomes one with himself after
death; the resurrection unites the dead poet with his youth. The
old man looks into the pool, and the image that he sees is a
younger "he."

Miraré ese que yo sea,
Para hallarle a la imagen de aquel mozo
A quien dijera adiós en tiempos
Idos, su juventud intacta
De nuevo, esperando, creyendo, amando.

(*RD.*, p. 253.)

Time is finally conquered, since the two ages of man are now one:
"la hermosura que el haber vivido / Pudo ser, unirá al alma / La
muerte así, en un presente inmóvil." The union of this new manifestation of the *desdoblamiento del yo* is now complete and non-
temporal, for it is a union of two shadows in another world:
"e iremos por el prado a las aguas, donde olvido ... fundirá en
una sombra nuestras sombras."

In the same way, the "other" is sought upon waking from a
dream in "La sombra":

Al despertar de un sueño, buscas
Tu juventud, como si fuera el cuerpo
Del camarada que durmiese
A tu lado y que al alba no encuentras.

(*RD.*, p. 261.)

Just as the youth of the poet was retrieved in resurrection in "El
éxtasis," the personification of the poet's youth is sought in the

body of the lover, but this time the figure of the "other" is not found, leaving the poet in his initial solitude, contrasting brusquely with the unified state that he found in the other world:

> Ahora ... ida también, es sólo
> Un vago malestar, una inconsciencia
> Acallando el pasado, dejando indiferente
> Al otro que tú eres, sin pena, sin alivio.
>
> (*RD.*, p. 261.)

The figure of youth as the "other" reaches its most complex formulation in the poem "Viendo volver," where the poet invents two totally different lives: one pertaining to himself as a youth, remaining young as the years pass, and the "other," the aging self, who returns to observe the static projection of the poet's own youth which is fictional but eternal:

> Irías, y verías
> Todo igual, cambiado todo,
> Así como tú eres
> El mismo y otro. Un río
> A cada instante
> No es él y diferente?
> ... ...
> Así, con pasmo indiferente,
> Como llevado de una mano,
> Llegarías al mundo
> Que fue tuyo otro tiempo,
> Y allí le encontrarías,
> Al tú de ayer, que es otro hoy

The poet continues to observe this earlier self, this "other," but imagines it as a future companion to relieve his solitude:

> Impotente, extasiado
> Y solo, como un árbol,
> Le verías, el futuro
> Soñando, sin presente,
> A espera del amigo,
> Cuando el amigo es él y en él le espera.

The companion is the poet in another epoch. The one desires the other, but both are one, each being the self in different stages

along the life continuum. The search is futile, for the poet seeks
the other using a mirror:

> Al verle, tú querrías
> Irte, ajeno entonces,
> Sin nada que decirle,
> Pensando que la vida
> Era una burla delicada,
> Y que debe ignorarlo el mozo hoy.
>
> (*RD.*, pp. 273-274.)

The poet remains silent. His earlier personification still waits
for the older self to complete the potential within the youth, the
earlier self.

BIBLIOGRAPHY

I. Editions of Cernuda's Works and Translations

A. Works

Perfil del aire. Cuarto suplemento de "Litoral." Málaga: Imprenta Sur, 1927.
La invitación a la poesía. Madrid: Ediciones "La Tentativa Poética," 1933.
Donde habite el olvido. Madrid: Editorial Signo, 1934.
El joven marino. Madrid: Colección "Héroe," 1936.
La realidad y el deseo. Madrid: Cruz y Raya, 1936.
Ocnos. London: The Dolphin Press, 1942.
Las nubes. Buenos Aires: Colección "Rama de Oro," 1943.
Como quien espera el alba. Buenos Aires: Editorial Losada, 1947.
Tres narraciones. Buenos Aires: Editorial Imán, 1948.
Ocnos. Segunda edición aumentada. Madrid: Colección Ínsula, 1949.
Variaciones sobre tema mexicano. México: Colección "México y lo mexicano," Porrúa y Obregón, 1952.
Poemas para un cuerpo. Málaga: Colección "A quien conmigo va," Imprenta Dardo, 1957.
Estudios sobre poesía española contemporánea. Madrid: Ediciones Guadarrama, 1957.
La realidad y el deseo. Tercera edición, corregida y aumentada. México: Colección "Tezontle," Fondo de Cultura Económica, 1958.
Pensamiento poético en la lírica inglesa (siglo XIX). México: Imprenta Universitaria, 1958.
Poesía y literatura. Barcelona: Seix Barral, 1960.
Desolación de la quimera. México: Joaquín Mortiz, 1962.
Ocnos. Tercera edición. Xalapa: Universidad Veracruzana, 1964.
La realidad y el deseo. Cuarta edición. México: Colección "Tezontle," Fondo de Cultura Económica, 1964.
Poesía y literatura II. Barcelona: Seix Barral, 1964.

II

Aldana, Francisco de. *Obras completas.* Madrid: Consejo Superior de Investigaciones Científicas, 1953.
Casalduero, Joaquín. *Cántico de Jorge Guillén.* Madrid and New York: Victoriano Suárez, 1953.

CERNUDA, LUIS. "Juan Ramón Jiménez," *Hijo Pródigo*, I, No 3 (June, 1943), pp. 148-156.

CIPLIJAUSKAITE, BIRUTÉ. *La soledad y la poesía española contemporánea*. Madrid: Colección Ínsula, 1962.

DOSTOYEVSKY, FYODOR. *The Brothers Karamazov*. trans., Constance Garnett. New York: The Modern Library.

ELIOT, T. S. *Selected Essays*. New York: Harcourt, Brace and Company, 1960.

————. "The Three Voices of Poetry," in *On Poetry and Poets*. London: Faber and Faber, 1957.

————. *Complete Poems and Plays*. New York: Harcourt, Brace and Company, 1952.

FERRATÉ, JUAN. *La operación de leer*. Barcelona: Seix Barral, 1962.

FITZMAURICE-KELLY, JAMES. (ed.). *The Oxford Book of Spanish Verse*. Oxford: The Clarendon Press, 1945.

HEIDEGGER, MARTIN. *Erläuterungen zu Hölderlins Dichtung*. Frankfurt am Main: V. Klostermann, 1951.

HÖLDERLIN, FRIEDRICH. *Selected Poems*, trans., J. B. Leishman. London: The Hogarth Press, 1954.

KAUFMANN, WALTER. *From Shakespeare to Existentialism*. Garden City: Doubleday Anchor Books, 1960.

LAÍN ENTRALGO, PEDRO. *Teoría y realidad del otro*. Madrid: Revista de Occidente, 1961.

LAING, R. D. *The Divided Self*. Chicago: Quadrangle Books, 1960.

————. *The Self and Others*. Chicago: Quadrangle Books, 1962.

LYNCH, WILLIAM F. *Christ and Apollo*. New York: Mentor Books, 1963.

MACHADO, ANTONIO. *Obras completas*. Madrid: Editorial Plenitud, 1957.

MARTZ, LOUIS L. *The Poetry of Meditation*. New Haven: The Yale University Press, 1955.

MUELLER, ELISABETH. *Die Dichtung Luis Cernudas*. Geneva: Librairie E. Droz, 1962.

MENCKEN, H. L. (ed). *A New Dictionary of Quotations*. New York: Alfred Knopf, 1946.

NERUDA, PABLO. *Obras completas*. Buenos Aires: Losada, 1956.

OLIVIO JIMÉNEZ, JOSÉ. *Cinco Poetas del Tiempo*. Madrid: Ínsula, 1964.

ONG, WALTER J. *The Barbarian Within*. New York: Macmillan and Company, 1962.

ORTEGA Y GASSET, JOSÉ. "Meditación del Escorial," in *Obras completas*. Madrid: Revista de Occidente, 1957, Vol. II.

PAZ, OCTAVIO. "Andando el tiempo." *Claridades literarias*, No. 2 (May, 1959).

PRESCOTT, W. H. *History of the Conquest of Mexico*. London: J. P. Lippincott, 1904.

RUSKIN, JOHN. *Modern Painters*. New York: Merrill and Baker, n. d.

SARTRE, JEAN PAUL. *Baudelaire*. Paris: Gallimard, 1947.

SHOEMAKER, SYDNEY. *Self-Knowledge and Self-Identity*. Ithaca: Cornell University Press, 1963.

SILVER, PHILIP. *Et in Arcadia Ego: A Study of the Poetry of Luis Cernuda*. London: Támesis Books Limited, 1965.

STRICH, FRITZ. *Der Dichter und die Zeit*. Bern: A. Francke, 1947.

SYPHER, WYLIE. *Loss of the Self in Modern Literature and Art*. New York: Random House, 1962.

UNTERECKER, JOHN (ed). *Yeats, A Collection of Critical Essays.* Englewood Cliffs: Prentice-Hall, 1963.

VALENTE, JOSÉ ÁNGEL. "Luis Cernuda y la poesía de la meditación," *La caña gris,* Nos. 6-8 (Autumn, 1962).

WICKERSHAM CRAWFORD, J. P. *Spanish Drama before Lope de Vega.* Philadelphia: University of Pennsylvania Press, 1937.

WRIGHT, GEORGE T. *The Poet in the Poem.* Berkeley: University of California Press, 1960.

YEATS, WILLIAM BUTLER. *Autobiography.* New York: Macmillan and Company, 1938.